ON THE LEVEL

Bob Mierisch completed a Master's Degree in Civil Engineering at the University of Adelaide in 1955. He joined the construction company A.W. Baulderstone Pty Ltd (now Baulderstone Hornibrook) in 1958, became its general manager in 1963 and was chief executive from 1972 until he retired in 1989. He maintained his association with the company as a non-executive director until March 2000. He was elected an Honorary Fellow of the Institution of Engineers Australia in 1991, the highest honour of his profession, and in 1994 was appointed a Member of the Order of Australia for service to the building and construction industry and to the community. In 1990 Bob Mierisch and his wife, Judy, established Kindalya, a small retreat centre at Stirling in the Adelaide Hills providing a ministry of hospitality to those seeking time out for rest, reflection and renewal of spirit.

ON THE LEVEL

*A story about
striving for openness
to build corporate strength*

Bob Mierisch

**Wakefield
Press**

Wakefield Press
17 Rundle Street
Kent Town
South Australia 5067

First published 2000

Copyright © Bob Mierisch, 2000

Cover designed by Dean Lahn, Lahn Stafford Design
Designed and typeset by Clinton Ellicott, Wakefield Press
Indexed by Bill Phippard, Professional Editing Services
Printed and bound by Hyde Park Press

National Library of Australia
Cataloguing-in-pubilcation entry

Mierisch, Bob.
On the level: a story about striving for openness to build corporate strength.

Includes index.
ISBN 1 86254 513 8.

1. Mierisch, Bob. 2. Baulderstone Hornibrook (Firm).
3. Construction industry – Australia – Moral and ethical aspects.
4. Entrepreneurs – Australia – Biography. I. Title.

338.7624092

For my family

Judy, Sue, Richard and Jane
who shared the story through all its shades
and for our grandchildren
Joana, James, Sally, Samantha, Sam and Madeleine

The lord of all the tricks of war surveyed
this fugitive and smiled: He said:
'Courage; my son has dug you out and saved you.
Take it to heart, and pass the word along;
fair dealing brings more profit in the end.'

Homer

CONTENTS

PREFACE

This book is a story about what it takes to build a successful, lasting enterprise. It is partly autobiographical, partly reflective. It is a record of what I have learnt and am still learning from my experiences in organisational life in business, industry, church and government. It encompasses both the strategic and the cultural but focuses mostly on culture, the roots that give life to an organisation. It is a story about making a journey, not about arriving.

Stories have gained a new lease of life as we enter a new millennium. In therapy, listening to a person's story and helping that person to hear their own story are frequently found to be a most helpful way towards healing. Listening to the ancient and modern stories of others is at the heart of reconciliation movements around the world.

Telling stories could be seen as the flip side of our obsession with change. Both are part of our scene. When I think about the world I entered when I graduated nearly 50 years ago, the material and physical elements of life and work are so vastly different. But when I ask myself what was important then in forming friendships, in working relationships or human motivation, I find no vast differences.

We live with this contradiction and the dilemmas and anxieties it brings with it. While global economic and technological forces conveyed through increasingly powerful government and business corporations seem more and more to be dictating the kinds of lives we live, and also increasing the competition faced by most businesses, at the same time more voices are demanding that all corporations rethink their obligations to the communities on which they are having such impact – the call is to raise the standards of their corporate ethics, care and citizenship.

Within this emerging market place, pursuit of quality has become an accepted bench-mark for today's customer-driven organisation – quality products and services. But there seems much less real emphasis on making quality the mark of the corporation. This also is a contradiction.

Striving for openness to build corporate strength is the pathway I chose to follow to combat these fragmenting influences which are constantly present in our organisations as in our world. This pathway has its own pitfalls and benefits. However, I hope the experiences recounted will open doors for readers, prompting questions about their own situations and roles in organisation life, and reflections on why certain decisions are made and the possible and probable consequences of alternative choices.

In telling my story, I have looked at the elements which make up an enterprise separately and in sequence. It is inevitable that such a study will take the reader on a sometimes convoluted pathway, with frequent stops to look at the same events and experiences from changed viewing points. If it seems like that, I hope that any repetition will enhance rather than tire, and function more like the recurring theme of a familiar symphony which adds to the experience by reminding us constantly that the individual movements are always embraced by the whole.

AUTHOR'S NOTE

The greatest part of my experience in organisations has been gained through employment with the construction group A. W. Baulderstone Holdings Pty Ltd so that while this is a personal story, it is also in part a company story from my point of view. I have appreciated the opportunity to continue to contribute to the company as a non-executive director over the last ten years and have made reference to one or two events in this time. However, almost all material is drawn from the period up to the end of 1989 when I retired as a full-time executive. I have not consulted with or involved any other person in the writing of this book and make no claims or inferences, nor express any expectations, about the present or future operations of the company.

A few words of explanation and definition are needed. Only the full names of two persons with whom I worked have been used – Bert Baulderstone, who founded Baulderstone and died in 1974, and David Lloyd-Thomas, adviser and mentor, who died in 1980. It was not appropriate to mention any other colleagues by name, but their participation, contribution and encouragement over the years we worked together are sincerely recognised. I have tried to be authentic and not pedantic in the use of gender; the fact is that construction is still a predominantly male industry and for this reason mostly male gender is used in the narrative. However, the sense is always gender inclusive.

I have had a little difficulty with definitions in two areas. The words organisation, enterprise, company, corporation are all to some extent interchangeable. As far as I have been able, I have chosen to use 'enterprise' as the general name for any productive unit (ie a business, a government department or utility, a charitable trust or not-for-profit institution, an industry association etc) have reserved 'company' for references to Baulderstone, and only used 'organisation' and 'corporation' when that seemed to convey the sense more simply.

Leader, manager, supervisor, executive are another group of words which have overlapping meanings, while in recent years there has been an increased disposition to focus on leader and discount the term manager. In this text, manager is the word most commonly chosen to depict the leader person in any team, group or unit of an enterprise. As for the previous case, other words are restricted to occasions where it is simpler to use them.

When quotations have been used from other sources, those sources are identified. Beyond this I wish, in particular, to acknowledge with warm appreciation the works of the following authors and educators for the contribution their thoughts and ideas have brought to my under-standing and development over a long period. I refer to James C Collins and Jerry I Porras, Peter F Drucker, Robert K Greenleaf, Robert R Blake and Jane Srygley Mouton. I am most grateful also to Titia Rutten and Peter Kelly for their allowing me to quote from their personal letters to me in 1998, to Helen O'Sullivan, Dr Billie Slater and Professor Lee Parker for their willingness to read the manuscript and their helpful comments, and to Wendy Graham for her care in typing it. Most recently I am much indebted to Michael Bollen for his careful, thoughtful editing and advice, and his support in bringing this story to publication.

Finally, this book is an expression of my deep gratitude to those colleagues who have been partners in learning, sharers of dreams and nurturers of an enduring culture we struggled to build on firm foundations. They have been labourers, tradesmen, plant operators, engineers, secretaries, administrators, couriers, project managers, executives, directors ... There are no restrictive qualifications for supporters. I hope this testimony of their involvement will help others to see new possibilities within themselves.

Bob Mierisch
February 2000

Part I

ORGANISATIONS AND LIFE

Quest for Authenticity

Baulderstone exists for those who have a stake in it and, in return, these stakeholders have a community of interest which supports the continuity of the Group.

From the Baulderstone Philosophy

Chapter 1

CHOOSING
PERSPECTIVE

Change is the only constant! Adapt to change in order to survive and live!
Change, change, change . . .

The incessant clamour of many a modern bell tower tolls its
singular, strident note till we are numbed by it. But it is only one note.
Might we not sometimes need to hear this bombardment as the ringing
of the small change and the short change, the seductive and manipu-
lative part-truth masquerading in the colours of a new dawning but
obscuring the whole day and night?

The ever-accelerating rate of change resulting from the impact of
scientific discovery on population, knowledge, distance, communi-
cations, employment, relationships and industrial production is part
of our world. In respect of these, every organisation will either adapt
or die, one way or another. Change is inescapable but it is not the
whole story.

We should be wary lest it thrust its pervading bias into every
thought and idea. We have seen the publication and acclaim of a flood
of best-sellers in the 1980s and 1990s on the themes of leadership,
values and effective human participation in organisational and institutional life. Suddenly, to these commentators on the productivity and
future of enterprises, people have become important. In many cases, the
emphasis is portrayed as something new – new skills and adaptability
necessary to cope with change and the information age, a new para-
digm for a new century.

I do not believe this is either correct or helpful. It exaggerates the
importance of now at the expense of the best experiences of survival
and progress in history. Surely it is more accurate and helpful to

acknowledge this recognition of the essential linkage between people and high productivity as a reawakening to those principles that change only little or slowly, that endure as the foundations of that which does change. My own journey in life and business has led me to this conclusion. It is a perspective gained by way of another pathway to that which I feel is implied in much of the writings and motivational urgings of this time.

These writings and urgings argue that, in order to succeed, leadership and values which sustain effective human participation can and must be added on to what has been useful, but deficient, in past 'management' practice. I rather suspect that the reverse is what is needed to produce services and benefits of lasting quality – **that leadership and values which sustain effective human participation need always to be the root stock onto which the changing requirements of the enterprise are to be grafted.**

I have been encouraged by the support given to this conclusion by James Collins and Jerry Porras in their book *Built to Last – Successful Habits of Visionary Companies*. In speaking of their intentions and discoveries as they conducted their six-year research study of large international businesses, they explained:

> We wanted to go beyond the incessant barrage of management buzz-words and fads of the day. We set out to discover the *timeless* management principles that have consistently distinguished outstanding companies. Along the way, we found that many of today's 'new' and 'innovative' management methods really aren't new at all. Many of today's buzz-words – employee ownership, empowerment, continuous improvement, TQM, common vision, shared values, and others – are repackaged and updated versions of practices that date back, in some cases, to the 1800s.

Perhaps it is, after all, the age of recycling!

In the semi-arid regions of Australia, there grows a remarkable tree called the scrub mallee. Unfortunately, its roots in particular (the celebrated mallee root) make marvellous firewood, so that after 200 years of scrub clearing for agriculture and fuelling paddle steamers, steam trains and home fires, little virgin scrub remains.

A few years ago, our grandson, James, who has a passion for reptiles, took me to Yookamurra, a small dry-land conservation park which contains a stand of undisturbed mallee. I felt ashamed of my ignorance about this native flora of my own land. I had walked in the mountain mist amongst towering redwoods in California and stood in awe at their majesty and their age – the diminishing rings of their great girths measuring off the years of modern history to before the birth of Christ. Now, half a world away, I stood shaded from the sun amongst scrub not much more than a tenth as tall. But, until then, I was not aware that under my feet the great mallee root system of this single stand of trees had shared its time with the redwoods; it was just as old, the same roots giving birth to many new generations of trunk and foliage.

Here, it seems, is a living parable for organisational life. What is above the ground is constantly being replaced, each generation of trunk and branch giving way to new growth for survival in the environment of the day – a symbol for the strategic initiatives and responses of the enterprise as it seeks to anticipate and compete in the ever-changing present. The roots below the ground create, feed and support the renewing of the visible tree. They are a symbol for the culture of the enterprise, the practices, standards, values and beliefs which give birth, life and confidence to successive generations of strategic direction and operation.

Like the scrub mallee, an enterprise is what is above the ground and what is below, what is immediately visible and what is not. Both parts are entwined and are strengthened or weakened by the influence of each on the other. Yet they are also distinct elements. One distinction is that the formulation of strategy usually rests with a small number of persons who have the position, skills, experience and insight to fulfil this critical task.

The maintenance of a strong, healthy, dynamic culture, however, requires supporters in all parts of the enterprise, a requirement which increases as the enterprise grows in size.

Chapter 2

INFLUENCES
WHICH SHAPE

I walked on the beach this morning with Judy, my wife and friend. It was warm, still and sunny, a wide flat beach where the shallow tide still meanders across the mangrove-studded sand for half a kilometre or so. A good place for crabs in season.

The tide was halfway out. Or was it halfway in? I thought aloud. Judy laughed. I knew immediately why. I always comment on the tide, never fail; she just has to wait for it. It's going out. No, it's coming in. I think! Its ebb and flow touches some unsung chord within me. Part of the whole scheme of things. Congruence. Contradiction.

Walking on the beach is a companionable thing to do after more than 40 years. I thought of the first year of our marriage when we moved to the new town of Elizabeth in 1956, a few months after the first residents arrived there. It was a flat, treeless former wheat field, with new houses creeping across it like that incoming tide, without street lights then, isolated from transport, peopled by migrants used to the closeness and services of crowded cities, muddy in winter, dusty in summer. A new beginning.

Elizabeth, 20 kilometres north of Adelaide, was a new venture for the State of South Australia, conceived to bring both life and work to a regional centre close to the city. It was brought into being with all the aspirations and promises of a second vision, 130 years after Colonel Light's vision for the City of Adelaide. Young and idealistic, the pioneering genes of my fourth generation Australian heritage stirred in my veins as I dreamed of the challenges ahead. We had much to learn, and we did!

Here I met Gwilym, the first of two Welshmen who were each to become in their separate ways trusted mentor and cherished friend. Our backgrounds could not have been more different.

My childhood and youth could genuinely be described as modest, ordinary and somewhat Victorian in character and influences. I had one brother. My father was away much of the time. He was, successively, country traveller, Second World War serviceman, long-term hospital patient. Then he and my mother divorced. Divorce in the 1940s was uncommon and shameful. It heightened my sense of duty and responsibility, and my independence, as I observed the courage and sacrifice with which my mother shaped a new life which enabled me, with the support of both my parents, to complete school and university.

Gwilym, 20 years my senior, was one of 12 children who grew up in the Welsh mining village of Maesteg through years of depression. The only one of his family to complete secondary school, he had been a mineworker, unemployed, supporter of the family through his skill with a billiard cue, shopkeeper, merchant navy man, torpedoed three times, decorated for bravery, migrant, technical clerk, preacher and pastor. He was an example to all of us, a friend whom hardship and injustice had failed to embitter, who has never stopped seeing life as opportunity. 'Memories live longer than dreams' is one of his credos.

Our first conversation occurred on a scorching summer afternoon shortly after he and his family had moved into the house across the back fence. He was merrily feeding a bonfire with the products of the clean-up of his new yard – there were no bush fires where he had come from! Gwilym, a great raconteur, had a story for every occasion. One has remained my favourite over the years, perhaps because bridges hold a special, even mystical, fascination for civil engineers. In any case, it was so for me. The story goes:

> Many years ago, passengers who travelled by train from Cardiff on the coast to Brechon, the historical Welsh capital in the central hill country, were required to change trains at a small village en route. Passengers arriving from Cardiff had to cross to the Brechon line by way of an old, cast-iron over-bridge.
>
> On this particular day, the porter on duty, Dai by name, was

irritable. His wife was away and he'd been looking forward to an early pint and a good feed at the local; but the afternoon train was late. So when it finally arrived, he walked impatiently up and down the platform urging the passengers in a strident tone: 'Over the bridge to Brechon! Over the bridge to Brechon!'

He almost smiled as the last person hurried by, only to be confronted by the belated opening of the last door in the last carriage. He watched in disgust as the wizened old lady climbed gingerly down the step, reached back inside and pulled out a battered tin trunk which clattered noisily to the platform.

She looked round, dazed by her exertion. That was before her eyes fell on Dai. She beamed with relief. 'Porter, can you please help me? How do I get to Brechon?'

Dai, frustrated, responded, 'Over the bridge to Brechon!'

'B . . . but, Porter', she stammered, 'I have this tin chest . . .'.

'Madam, I don't care if you have a brass arse! It's over the bridge to Brechon!'

Like that old lady, I understand the feeling of being thrust and compelled, sometimes reluctantly, to walk in a particular direction, of there being only one way to go.

The twin bridges of my adult life have led, not to Brechon, but along the intertwined pathways of my search for meaning and its expression in my experience in and with organisations. The erratic wanderings of this person's spirit in search of the meaning of his life is another story. It is not a subject for this book, except to acknowledge its constant influence on my organisational endeavours, and its contribution to learning from success and error.

For me, this personal journey springs from the summons to be Christian, a decision which I faced with reluctance and came to tentatively as a young man. Neither have I continued to follow that way without resistance, doubt and disappointment. But given my time over again, I would not choose another path, for I have also discovered that faith, hope and love have the power to enrich and deepen life's experiences and relationships. In this, I have been greatly encouraged and supported by my family, close friends and some treasured authors whose writings have brought stimulation, insight and new ideas.

The search for meaning as a human being does not end. It certainly does not end in certainty! But the journey is teaching me to hold with greater confidence and stillness the absence of certainty which is part of being human – the sometimes perplexing, sometimes exhilarating events of living and working which are occasionally congruent but more often paradoxical and contradictory. Expressed another way, following this path has given me roots. Through this I have become convinced that this need for roots is more than personal or individual. Community and corporate values also need roots if they are to be more lasting than a vase of cut flowers.

In an address given in 1989, I explained my reasons:

> *The Proud Tower*, by Pulitzer Prize-winning American historian Barbara Tuchman, draws a fascinating picture of events in England, the United States, France and Germany in the turbulent 25 years preceding the First World War – ie the period which started 100 years ago when western society was grappling with the influences of Darwin, Freud, the Anarchist Movement, and other philosophies which came to challenge its very roots and beliefs. And this was happening concurrently with the arrival of the telephone, auto-mobile, radio, cinema and electricity.
>
> I was left with the feeling that the changes thrust upon society in that period were as dramatic as anything with which the twentieth century has had to cope, a view which is somewhat contrary to that so often expressed today. But I also felt that much of the instability, loss of purpose, feeling of meaninglessness, the need for instant gratification in our century have their origins in the rejection of the old sources through which the growth and development of the human spirit was nurtured, without replacing them with alternative sources of nourishment.
>
> The way we act is inexorably the consequence of what we believe and value in the core of our being whether we are conscious

of those values or acknowledge and can articulate them or not. As a society, we have survived through this century on those diminishing resources of the spirit drawn from earlier ages. But will we survive through the next? I wonder if the turn in management thinking and expression by business leaders here and elsewhere towards such issues as values, trust, time to think and meditate, vision, ethics and relationships is not the beginning of a recognition that our world, our lives, our businesses will not work in the long term without the renewal of a relevant spiritual foundation.

There is a wide consensus that excellence, quality and service are to be the hallmarks of our products and businesses of the future. If we purchase a high-quality motor car we expect it to be without flaws, that it will last. Enterprises which are able to deliver excellent, lasting products or services will require congruent values to nourish their strategies, systems, processes and relationships. To believe otherwise is simply to place trust in false hopes.

Values which are rooted in our convictions and experiences from the whole of life help us to keep in focus more of that whole when we look at our enterprises and institutions. They encourage us to keep on asking how the parts fit together within that whole, to keep on testing for authenticity. And herein lies a particular opportunity for enterprises to contribute to combating the growing fragmentation which is felt by so many of the world's communities as we enter the new century. Others in our time have also been pointing this way.

In *The New Realities*, Peter Drucker explains how he sees this opportunity emerging:

Thirty years ago, the English scientist and novelist C.P. Snow talked of the 'two cultures' of contemporary society. Management, however, fits neither Snow's 'humanist' nor his 'scientist'. It deals with action and application; and its test are results. This makes it a technology. But management also deals with people, their values, their growth and development and this makes it a humanity. So does its concern with, and impact on, social structure and the community. Indeed, as everyone has learned who, like this author, has been working with managers of all kinds of institutions for long years, management is deeply involved in spiritual concerns – the nature of man, good and evil.

Management is thus what tradition used to call a liberal art – 'liberal' because it deals with the fundamentals of knowledge, self-knowledge, wisdom, and leadership; 'art' because it is practice and application. Managers draw on all the knowledge and insights of the humanities and the social sciences – on psychology and philosophy, on economics and history, on the physical sciences and ethics. But they have to focus this knowledge on effectiveness and results – on healing a sick patient, teaching a student, building a bridge, designing and selling a 'user-friendly' software program.

For these reasons, management will increasingly be the discipline and the practice through which the 'humanities' will again acquire recognition, impact, and relevance.

Robert Greenleaf's *Servant Leadership* was published some years earlier. He writes:

For years I made the strongest pleas I could for our major institutions to become affirmative (as opposed to passive or reactive) servants of society. In 1974, the first unequivocal response came to me, saying 'we would like to know how to be that kind of institution'.

This response did not come from where the casual observer might guess – a church, a university, a hospital, a social agency. It came from where I expected it, from a business, a large multinational business. I expected this not because I impute any special virtue to business as such, but because, as I know institutions, businesses are least lulled to complacency by idealistic pretensions and the support of sentiment, and they have fewer professional hang-ups than the others.

This has also been my experience. My greatest learning and encouragement about how people work together in organisations irrespective of their purpose has come from business. It is from this source that I have come to understand the kinds of conditions which will continually yield real improvements in an enterprise's performance and results while enhancing satisfaction and fulfilment amongst its people. The same conditions will also encourage an enterprise to integrate into its thinking and planning the impact on and contribution it makes to the community of which it is part.

Chapter 3

UNLIKELY
SURVIVOR

TOWARDS EXCELLENCE: The A.W. Baulderstone Story is both a biography and a company history; it is the story of Bert Baulderstone and the company he founded. It sets out to explain why Bert's small building firm, a comparatively late starter in South Australia, grew to become the largest building company in the State.

It is a success story, though not simply a celebratory one. Any success that Bert and his company achieved was the result of extraordinary ability on their part and a great deal of painstaking effort, much of it in the face of problems that threatened the company's very existence. Indeed, the story is one of problems constantly being confronted, with every successful solution throwing up more problems in turn requiring resolution.

These words by Peter Donovan from the flyleaf of the corporate history he was asked to write provide one perspective on what I will call the Baulderstone experience. A short collection of historical events tends to support that perspective while also suggesting that Baulderstone's survival was *always* unlikely in its first 40 years.

Bert Baulderstone battled physical restrictions all his life. Born in 1906, cataracts impaired his vision from age 14. He suffered rheumatic fever at 17 and thereafter was obliged to take angina tablets regularly. By 1960 he was almost blind and chose to undergo pioneering cataract surgery in 1961 and 1962. The surgery was successful in restoring 75 per cent of his sight, but only after the intense pain and curtailed activity of a two-year convalescence which greatly restricted his role in the business.

Personal sorrow and loss also claimed his attention and time just as the business was gaining momentum. In 1950, his first wife of 21 years died; his youngest and closest brother, who worked for him as administrator died three years later. Then, in 1961, his younger daughter died tragically, leaving a young family.

Bert was mostly a loner and something of an outsider. He was a late starter compared to most of those to whom he became a challenging competitor, and was certainly seen by some initially as an upstart. Few thought he or his company would succeed and the doubters and knockers lasted for four decades. It took 20 years for him to be invited to the luncheon inner-circle of Adelaide's ten or so principal builders, yet now only two of the ten companies then represented are still in business. These two, by choice, have remained much as they were then.

Before 1983, Baulderstone was starved of any source of significant new investment or financial backing. It had to rely on and operate within the capitalisation of its own efforts. This had been so from the beginning in 1938, when Bert started out as a labour-only, bricklaying subcontractor with no assets. When he died in 1972, his family home and private affairs were still principal assets of the business. Bert never had a financial adviser of high calibre and it is interesting to speculate on how the company's history might have been different if he had.

Due to inexperience more than rank incompetence, Baulderstone scraped past bankruptcy in the early 1940s, in 1961 when perhaps a half-dozen competitors went to the wall, in 1972, and again in 1980 when it survived another anxious time.

South Australia, one of the least populated regions in Australia, the driest and the least blessed with natural resources, was away from the mainstream of national development. It was an unsympathetic launching pad for national business. It was more difficult to attract construction staff with breadth of experience, more difficult to build a track record.

The struggle portrayed by these events is part of the whole, part of what makes the Baulderstone experience real. Perhaps we were unusually slow learners. But is there an enduring enterprise which hasn't suffered, or which doesn't need to be constantly alert to human frailty? Every enterprise finds it hard to learn from its own experience, and even more difficult to pass on the lessons learned from one generation of leaders to the next. And then those lessons must be accepted!

Dreams, initiatives, vigour, enthusiasm ... mistakes, pain, heartsearching ... headstrong defiance ... courage, compassion, reward, achievement, fun ... Life's like that, life that survives. It's like that too for organisations; it's the pattern for enterprises that survive. There will always be exceptions, but not many. I've looked and read, I've listened to those who have worked for others, I've worked closely one way or another with three international corporations. I still don't see many exceptions. Experience and business leadership are not one-directional. It's not just a matter of ever onwards and upwards provided only that we 'believe' more.

We will do well in our businesses and societies to remember events across the globe in the 1980s. Many joined the bandwagon of acclaim. The entrepreneurs (so called) were the heroes and the models for a new age. Exponential growth in business and wealth was possible. To be a winner, you needed vision and courage to dream and dare, a willingness to take initiative and risks. We could create the markets, create the future.

How seductive are the half-truths? Australia had its heroes and its newsmakers – the mass media and the business journals endlessly sang their praises. But where are these enterprises now which were built by those who were mostly paper-shufflers? What did most of them build but houses of cards? The risks they took were clothed in other people's money. Time, in this case not a very long time, showed all this to be dangerous nonsense.

Just occasionally, a business motivated and channelled by exceptional insight and technical brilliance, and usually enjoying some good fortune in its timing, will harness the conditions of the day to yield extraordinary success in a short time. But the high-fliers of the 1980s did not build businesses such as these.

This book is mostly about what has been learnt in the business I know best. It describes one pathway which was taken towards the goal of building an excellent company – where progress is determined by measuring improvement in the quality of performance and the level of achievement. I acknowledge that there are other pathways, and we can learn from them all.

There are no perfect formulas but there are two things I have come to understand from my experience over 40 years. I am convinced of their soundness without reservation:

- **Every enterprise, business or other, is capable of substantial, lasting, ongoing improvement and the effort to create the conditions that generate and sustain that improvement is worth it.**
- **The values and principles that underpin those generating and sustaining conditions change little.**

When I joined Baulderstone in 1958, I was really beginning a search for authenticity, for a congruence between work and my largely untested beliefs, ideas and ambitions about life. Gradually, experience moulded and shaped these thoughts into convictions, values and principles that I was able to articulate. As I look at the company now, very different in form and scope, the same values and principles are no less needed. They were planted in the way Bert went about building his business; I see them also in the diverse patterns of human history.

The Baulderstone experience (together with others referred to in chapter 22) provide a real-life example to examine and test the soundness of certain values and principles. Over the 50 years since Baulderstone's establishment, methods, processes, attitudes, technology in the building and construction industry changed in line with the dramatic changes in society. During those years, Baulderstone moved from the founder–leader phase, through the turbulent transition to leadership by others and the trial of different systems of control, to the shaping of an enterprise that has grown to claim a place amongst the leading constructors in Australia. Its story, therefore, has the potential to be useful and helpful to a wide audience – students, young entrepreneurs starting out, and all learners in business enterprises. Further, the particular circumstances that existed at the time of Bert

Baulderstone's death expand this audience to include government and not-for-profit organisations.

Bert died at a time when the company was struggling to survive the consequences of significant losses from an ill-founded venture into the remote north-west of Western Australia. As a result, the company was strapped for cash and credit, while a large part of its assets were still entangled with the affairs of Bert's family and estate where control of 90 per cent of the shares resided. Not surprisingly, the family was courted to sell; but in the end there was only one tangible bid – a rock-bottom offer. No-one would have blamed them had they accepted it. No member of Bert's immediate family worked for the company, and the family would at least have something, small though it was, to show as benefit from Bert's labours. Against this, the odds on company survival were low, and the risk of losing everything was real.

This record of learning from experience can be written only because the family decided to back the employees. They believed that this is what Bert would have wanted, and what he would have done. The family–employee partnership that resulted was a partnership of good faith solely. It provided the company with no source or reserves of capital from any of its primary stakeholders; the future would only be won by securing the commitment of the employees. Government and not-for-profit organisations face a similar challenge in their search for the improvements in performance which the community is demanding of the former, and which are being thrust upon the latter by the constraints of diminishing financial support.

Chapter 4

OPENNESS
IS THE YEAST

From an often turbulent experience, I have learnt that the most universal essential for establishing enduring, high-quality performance and fulfilment in an enterprise is that conditions are created to sustain **a sufficient level of openness and trust** between its members and parts. There are, however, two qualifications which restrict this conclusion's universal application. It is a claim made about enterprises which intend to stay in business or service for the long term, and it applies to enterprises where performance and fulfilment are genuine intentions of both the enterprise and its people.

Seventeen years after starting with Baulderstone, I committed to paper what I saw as the company's reason for being. My objective was to win increased depth and strength of commitment from our people through the increased understanding that could only come from being open about these ideas. At about the same time, I started to make bread.

Bread-making is a useful illustration for thinking about openness. After an initial burst of success, I had trouble with my bread. Flat bread is not very appetising however wholesome the ingredients. I discovered eventually that the warming-oven was too hot for proving the yeast; I was pushing it too hard and it was dead before it had done its work. Quicker yeast certainly did not yield faster bread. Like yeast, the conditions for openness must be encouraging enough to get started, but its working cannot be accelerated outside the limits of its own growing conditions. Openness will not be given where there is no trust, and trust will not start to develop until there is some openness. Openness can never be assumed or demanded. Like yeast, it can only be grown.

The best-known, most appetising picture of bread is the whole loaf. My own taste buds respond particularly to the whole crusty loaf, and perhaps there's another lesson in that, somewhere. The yeast pervades the whole, but the baker must also know about the different flours, the milk, the water, the sugars, the seasonings. Openness, or its absence, pervades an organisation – its purpose, its leadership, the participation of its people, its learning, its quality and its integrity. To examine the parts separately is necessary for understanding, but they do not exist separately. Purpose spawns leadership and leadership strengthens or undermines purpose. Quality is a product of learning and participation.

All learning is a journey. The struggle to put it into practice adds authenticity. Most of us who start, grow, rebuild, maintain and lead organisations have quite heavy feet of clay. Too much emphasis on the end result or a great idea can convey false expectations about giant steps to success. To some, a giant step becomes an excuse for never taking any step. Some others are tempted to take that giant step without preparation, fall on their faces and never get up again.

When, however, I listen to a friend talking about his or her experiences of living, I am always encouraged; encouraged to move on, take a small step, even a large step. Encouragement is a leader's obligation. Courage is, like the word, embedded in encouragement. Even the courage to be open.

Part 2

REASON FOR BEING

Openness about Purpose

Because we intend to be in business over the long term, we are committed to the development of distinctive capabilities and professional competence so that our customers receive the best value for service in the market. Our aim is to be known for outstanding physical and financial performance, for the quality of our people and for the strength and creativity of our relationships with customers, employees, shareholders and associated enterprises and authorities.

Chapter 5

DREAMS AND
VISIONS

In 1970 Baulderstone put up a signpost. It read 'TOWARDS EXCELLENCE'. It appeared as a banner on the company newsletter, declaring to our employees, customers and associates the direction in which we wanted to go. This was probably seen as presumptuous by some inside and outside the company, and as mere words by others. But I had been grasped by the notion of building an excellent enterprise, and this held sway over any reticence about the glibness of 'slogans'. It held sway because it was more than a slogan; it was underpinned by a decade of searching. It was an important step to take in spite of my then limited understanding of what it really involved. Its continuing presence at the company's masthead confirms that importance.

By 1975 I felt that I needed more than two words to test my ideas and aspirations. I needed a brighter light on the far hill. After five years of facing up and rebuilding, my thinking was again being buffeted and clouded, this time by a changing industry and society. By this time, I had found writing down ideas and thoughts was a useful discipline for sorting out substance from waffle. If I couldn't write it down, was there anything there worth expressing? But if I *could* write down what I believed was really important about the kind of enterprise we were trying to build, I could look at it, test it and understand its fundamental elements. Then I would be equipped to lead my immediate colleagues through the same process and later share it with other employees.

This is how the Baulderstone Philosophy first came to be written 37 years after Bert had started his business. It had taken a long time to come to this point. It does not need to take so long. But we were learning by trial and error. There wasn't much help available then for enterprise-building in a small regional city, neither books nor advice.

We were also learning how to run a growing business. Neither Bert nor I had come from families with a business history, where some of the essentials might have rubbed off as we grew up. Those in the business and professional community who did have experience to impart displayed little interest in a small builder struggling to grow.

It is, however, these sorts of circumstances that make the journey the learning experience. Ideas emerge, take shape, suffer setback and are taken up again. Somehow, there is enough support in spite of the trials and errors, enough for the enterprise to survive.

The Baulderstone Philosophy expressed the company's reason for being through words that describe purpose and the values or beliefs which underpin that purpose. These words are used intentionally and not loosely, for the meaning we give to words is critical to communicating understanding. 'Vision' is a term that became popular in the 1980s. It has become over-used, and so requires definition. I think of an enterprise's vision statement as defining that goal which the enterprise expects to reach within a measurable time. Beyond that a new vision will emerge.

Vision has a strong strategic emphasis. In contrast, the light on the far hill is not a mark to be reached, but one which illuminates each successive vision. That light includes our dreaming. To dream is to be human. Not to dream is to deny the potential of our humanity. Dreams which spring from our latent and partly formed longings, ambitions, gifts and talents have the power to shape our future and lead us towards achievement that fulfils the individual persons we are.

This kind of dream is part of our reason for being. Reason for being always exists in an enterprise whether it is written down or not. What is practised gradually moulds itself into oral tradition.

In 1938 Bert, keen to follow his own star, left his uncles' business to begin contracting on his own account. His bicycle, bag of bricklayers' tools and £30 were his only tangible assets.

By the time I joined Bert's company 20 years later it had become a diverse, trade-based, medium-sized builder with about 400 employees. To increase his control over labour in order to maintain high-quality workmanship and timely performance, Bert had established a range of specialist trade subsidiaries to supplement the basic structural trades. As a result, the company payroll included carpenters, bricklayers, skilled and unskilled labourers, riggers, benders and fixers of steel reinforcement, concrete workers, joiners for manufacture and fixing, solid plasterers, fibrous plasterers for manufacture and fixing, plumbers, hot water mechanics, painters, electricians, plant operators and maintenance mechanics.

I am sure that Bert had no grand plan when he started out. He was motivated simply by the restless stirring of his confidence in his own ability and the recognition that he would always be the junior in the family business of his uncles. His dream was undefined. Yet it did not stay that way as he built his company, leading from the front through his thinking, planning and untiring physical effort and enthusiasm to keep the jobs moving. I have listened to his foremen, in particular, talk of past days and experiences – of Bert driving all night to deliver supplies to country jobs and working all day, of the comradeship where no-one knocked off till the day's task was finished, of their admiration for his knowledge, his building methods and his generosity.

Bert's dream was taking shape. Standards and practices which were valued were becoming a tradition that could be recognised:

- a company which was strong and growing
- a reputation for the highest quality of workmanship
- a genuine concern for his employees
- the personal example of a wider view through support given to charity, community and industry groups.

Intense personal loyalty to Bert stood out above all else in any conversation with a long-serving employee. 'Bert attracted this loyalty because of his high integrity, his common touch, and his personal interest in the welfare of his men and that of their families', wrote Peter Donovan. He quietly gave employees assistance to establish their first homes, and helped out in times of illness. He initiated communal events such as a generous Christmas function with its special gift for everyone, as well as a social club, sporting teams, and a superannuation fund.

So long as Bert was physically present and active, the values which underpinned his dream for his company were on display. Oral tradition provided identification, direction and shared commitment. But two weaknesses began to appear. From the employees' perspective, identification and commitment were shared only as trusted and valued employees, for that is how they saw themselves. Preserving the ethos of the business belonged to the boss. As well, when I listened to some of these employees in that first year with the company, it was from the past, not the present, that the stories came – Bert, by then, was not so much in the present.

Chapter 6

DREAMS ARE
FRAGILE

Last night I had a dream. It was very vivid. Many images, I can remember that much. But what was it about? Damn it! It's gone. This is a common personal experience. It is also an allegory for enterprises. The dream which gives the enterprise its reason for being is very fragile if it is only held – really held – by one person. It can be gone in a puff of wind.

It was almost like that when I joined Baulderstone. Bert's dream was disintegrating, though I was too new to everything to recognise it at the time. Later I was to come to understand just how crucial to success such awareness and alertness are – to be able to read the signs, to anticipate the consequences. Bert's dream was disintegrating under the combined impact of his deteriorating health, the absence of alternative leadership, an unwise appointment and a change in market conditions. Every enterprise, regardless of size, is vulnerable to such stresses at some time or times in its existence.

In the latter half of the 1950s Bert became increasingly concerned about his failing eyesight and the possibility of impending blindness. In addition, I am sure that the toll of personal tragedy and the fatigue of his demanding years of company-building had taken some of the edge from his vigour. His other employees included competent site foremen, a handful of roving supervisors and a small office staff. They were strong on loyalty, trade knowledge and skill but, apart from Bert and his 'little black book' of productivity records, there was no estimating experience appropriate to the size of the jobs now being sought, no understanding of control. There were no leaders ready to share the task of building the company, or even operating it successfully at the size and diversity to which it had already grown, perhaps overgrown.

In the absence of available leaders amongst existing employees, Bert had appointed an engineer with some industry experience but no contracting experience. He was not unknown to Bert because ten years earlier, while at university, he had used his surveying knowledge to help set out a long curved wall on the Adelaide Boys High School, a job which lifted the company into a significantly larger size of contract. But if he was not unknown, he was not known either. Appointed at the beginning of 1957, he was promoted to director and assistant manager after only five months and given full responsibility for the office and, more significantly, for estimating, the leading edge for any construction business.

In retrospect, it can only be seen as a decision taken in desperation. The new director indulged, without Bert's supervision, in a price-cutting rampage without any comprehension of the consequences. This practice sent several competitors out of business and was almost the death of Baulderstone. The financial results for this period illustrate the point. In the four financial years 1958 to 1962, small profits each year totalled £47,000; these were followed by declared losses of £97,000 in the next two years. There is no doubt that the losses had been incurred earlier and declaration deferred for the benefit of bankers until the company's crisis had passed.

Readers should be alert to, more than critical of, the errors of judgement made in this short period of company history. Stories of the fickleness of health and life, expansion beyond the level of leadership development and operational competence, and placing too much responsibility and confidence in the hands of untested recruits line the pages of every corporate history. I have too often strayed down these same paths to my considerable heartache and discomfort to be critical of others, and I have seen it happen in each of the successful international corporations with which I have had an association, sometimes resulting in huge financial losses.

This experience might appear to point more to what needs to be learned about good and bad business decisions and practices than it does to the fragility of a founder's dream. However, the two are inseparably entwined. Bert, says the company history, 'admitted to making many mistakes, but rarely made the same mistake twice'. Due to this capacity to be honest with himself and to learn, his business was continuously successful until 1957, as illustrated by its profitability and growth (achieved through the reinvestment of earnings). A key factor in this success had been the ability to perform better than competitors, a factor critically dependent in those labour-intensive days on the sustained high productivity of his workforce.

Sustained high productivity had been possible because of the 'culture of respect' on which Bert had been building his company. It was the outcome of his twin concerns for his people and for quality. He would never have claimed to have been the perfect boss, and he certainly imposed on some of his employees on occasions, but he never treated his employees as pawns. His respect for them was genuine. His commitment to high quality showed respect for their skills, and pride in their mutual achievements enhanced self-respect.

This culture of respect which had been growing through the years was put at risk by the same errors of judgement which almost scuttled the company.

Chapter 7

PICKING UP
THE PIECES

It takes longer to build than to knock down. Even longer to rebuild. This seems to be almost universally true.

After about two years, in 1960, Bert started to share increasingly with me the task of picking up the pieces of his company and his dream. This was a challenging and unexpected opportunity for me, but an extraordinary act of courage and good faith by him so soon after his first near disastrous experience of recruitment and delegation.

I did not have any great dream of the future when I came to Baulderstone. I was even further from any grand purpose than Bert when he had started on his own. I joined as a way of escape from my previous position in the public sector.

I have come to know many dedicated public servants and services, but my early experience was short of this kind. Halfway through my university studies, I gained a paid cadetship with an engineering utility. Its conditions included two years of bonded full-time service in return for two years of paid study time. When I decided that I wanted to undertake an additional year's study to complete a Master's Degree, I expected to take leave without pay to do it. However, I was granted this leave only on the condition that I agree to my bonded full-time service being extended to three years after the completion of that leave. It was not an ideal way to build loyalty to the organisation.

Those three years in the engineering design office felt a little like serving a sentence. My theoretical engineering knowledge gained some consolidation and reinforcement but my spirit was being crushed by the atmosphere of non-achievement, the frustration of being controlled by the system and a general inclination by many to do as little as possible.

I was fearful that if I stayed longer than my bond demanded, I could not help but take on the same attitudes. I started looking for other positions immediately I was free, making two applications without success.

It was third time lucky! Getting a job with Baulderstone was my good fortune and would become my working life. I was appointed as a site engineer on the first stage of a large hospital project, well and truly the biggest and structurally most demanding building contract Baulderstone had yet undertaken. My responsibilities were mundane – survey and set-out work and scheduling steel reinforcement for bending hardly tested my extra years of study. But for the first time in more than three years I was surrounded by fresh air and energetic people. I felt a surge of enthusiasm and adventure.

I was as green as they come. Two pieces of educated paper but no field experience, no knowledge of building work and building trades as distinct from engineering, no family business background, and my participation in organisations was limited to church and sporting groups. Yet, there were a few building blocks for the future lying around. I had experienced the debilitating and pervasive influence of a negative culture in that design office (even if I couldn't have described it in those words back then). I had seen first hand its impact on performance. If I did not yet know what I wanted, I knew that this was something I did not want.

Another block came from a completely different quarter. The Sunday School teacher I best remembered from my early teen years had worked for an industrial firm. Later, during the nationwide coal strike in 1949, he had been put off just before Christmas and I had observed the anxiety and distress felt, as well as the courage shown, by him and his young family. Since that time, I had taken notice of reports which came my way occasionally about how some enterprises treated their employees indifferently or worse. These impressions were working at my sense of fairness and idealism – I did want something different, and better.

There was a third building block. Notwithstanding my inexperience, reserved temperament and relatively narrow and sheltered background, I felt at home with my new colleagues: down-to-earth, no frills and airs, salt-of-the-earth Australians. For this I am eternally grateful to my farmer uncles and adult cousins. With no father living at home, I had spent numerous school vacations working on their farms. They added lightness and breadth to my growing up through their generosity, fun and laughter, acceptance and practical tuition.

Because I felt comfortable with these practical men who had become my new workmates, I very quickly came to respect the considerable engineering intuition of Bert and the best of his foremen. On the few occasions I travelled with Bert in the country, I was fascinated by his stories of building jobs and characters. I admired the understanding he showed and the methods he and his men had used to overcome structural difficulties in complex demolition and rebuilding tasks, preserving the structural soundness of what was to be kept. This engineering intuition and a direct approach to solving problems contrasted dramatically with the often pedantic, rank-pulling rigidity of some professional engineering inspectors in those days.

The questions I asked were answered practically. I recall Tom, Bert's senior general foreman on my first job, explaining building details by drawing full size sketches with his three-foot tradesman's rule on the site-hut bench where I was working. These colleagues knew much more about many things than I did, and in their field it would always be so. From this introduction, the embryonic idea of harnessing effective participation began to form.

None of these emerging pieces of my thinking and experience were in conflict with the values on which Bert had been building his business. That is undoubtedly what provided the cement which gradually bonded an improbable marriage of very different backgrounds and personalities into a lasting partnership.

Bert salvaged his fragmenting company and dream in the only way he knew how, by taking up the reins again. The investment of his own past generosity and trustworthiness gained for him enough financial support from friends and business associates, as well as his bank, to survive. In spite of the difficulties, he did not discard his foundation convictions. Quality of workmanship was not sacrificed and he did not make his employees pay for his mistakes.

For several years Bert nurtured his new recruit by providing encouragement, opportunity and advancement. He had found someone who understood his dream and with whom he could begin to share it. A small step was therefore taken in the direction of openness. With more confidence this time, he was able to step back from the front line, take the many months needed for the surgery which gave him back his sight, and thereafter to give much of his experience and energy to leadership in professional, industry, sporting and community projects.

Chapter 8

IN PURSUIT OF UNDERSTANDING

Actions and leadership example, not words, create purpose.

Written words can only reinforce values and beliefs which have already been demonstrated. They are useful in strengthening purpose by fostering increased understanding and enhancing learning, and also in the induction of new employees. They become an increasingly necessary reinforcement as an organisation grows in size and diversity. But they can never replace example.

The five years between the adoption of the masthead declaration TOWARDS EXCELLENCE in 1970 and the writing of the Baulderstone Philosophy in 1975 were a crucible of learning. What actually occurred in that period is described more fully in Part 3 of this book but its impact was critical in the company's clarification and strengthening of its roots.

As had happened at the beginning of the 1960s for Bert, picking up the pieces was the nature of personal and company experience in the early 1970s. The process of organisation development, which was only just in its infancy, was suspended in 1972, replaced by a fight for company survival. My grand notion of building an excellent enterprise had taken a severe credibility battering because I had created expectations which had not been fulfilled.

We had shared some of our vision for the future with all managers and supervisors and introduced training which would prepare them for greater involvement – but while this was occurring, the wheels of the business were starting to fall off from more earthy, immediate pressures related to growth, matching experience and competition. When this happens deep-seated scepticism about new ideas gains strength.

The company wrestled with the consequences of my inexperience. When the storm of crisis had abated, in spite of feelings of nervousness and tentativeness, I determined to start building again, but this time with a stronger and more realistic commitment to see that we did things better.

As I reflect on that struggle, I recognise that its outcome was more actions and less words. Experience had taught that the bias must always be that way. If there were to be more words later, to increase understanding and involvement, then they must be accompanied by even more actions. First, it was necessary to rebuild confidence and trust in the company's leadership by performance. This did not mean focusing all our efforts on business strategy and efficiency of construction operations at the expense of building the company, for this would be an internal contradiction. It meant doing those things with which our people could identify immediately and which would lay the groundwork for a new thrust of company-building in the second half of the 1970s.

It was against this background and in the midst of significant moves for social and industrial change in South Australia that the first statement of Baulderstone Philosophy was written and accepted by the executive team and the board. We did not make it available to other staff for another three years.

The philosophy sought to encapsulate and explain the roots of this emerging enterprise. Its six themes – a wider view, quality of life, complexity and teamwork, leadership and partnership, profit, performance and measurement – were, in fact, sub-themes supporting the dominant values which had been part of the company from its beginning; respect for people and quality of workmanship pervade them all.

Paradoxically, respect and quality are not respecters of boundaries. Genuine respect for people cannot be restricted just to those within an enterprise while disregarding the wider relationships with customers, associates and the community in which that enterprise operates. If boundaries to respect are imposed by the actions of the enterprise, then the respect for and between the people within it will also be diminished.

This is not a statement of misplaced idealism; it simply recognises the reality of human experience. Neither does such recognition claim that we will always practise, or be able to practise, such universal respect; but it does remind us that we acknowledge and value the wholeness which is inherent in respect and that we will work to create conditions in our company which support this ideal and help all of us move in that direction in the way we work together.

The same applies to quality. A commitment to quality pervades every action, operation and relationship or its omission in one part inevitably produces flaws in another. Excellence, like perfection, is not an achievable state, but willingness to be measured against the highest standard we can conceive is the path and the motivation towards continuous improvement.

The company's commitment to and adoption of teamwork as a way of life grew out of experience. It had a personal thread which echoes the saying that 'necessity is the mother of invention'! Chance and opportunity thrust me into a position of leading the business in spite of significant gaps in my knowledge and experience. I was particularly conscious of two of these. Construction and trade practice needed to get the physical work done was one; accounting and financial knowledge the other. I had no choice but to rely on others and look for ways to work with them so that we would learn from each other in order that responsibility could be exercised and adequate control maintained.

Another thread came from external factors. Pressures inherent in the process of constructing commercial and engineering projects, particularly up to that time, pointed to a choice for or against teamwork. These sectors of construction comprise essentially one-off projects. Each new project started with a new customer with new expectations, a new management group within the company (eg project manager, foreman, administrator, engineer), a new group of designers and customers' representatives (eg architect, consulting engineer, quantity surveyor) and a new mix of trade labour and subcontractors. Few other industries are required to cope with such a range of continuous variations in the production process. The difficulties are compounded by changes in production location – each new project is at a new site and all are remote from a central office.

BAULDERSTONE PHILOSOPHY

(The first statement, 1975)

The Baulderstone Group exists for those who have a stake in it and not vice versa. Conversely, our stakeholders have a community of interest to preserve their common existence, which is expressed through the continuity of the Company.

We do not exist alone. Our Company is an important element in the structure of our society. We accept our responsibility to contribute through the quality of our products, our organisation culture and our relationships to the building up of society and not to breaking it down. We also accept this responsibility in the industry of which we are part.

We believe that the quality of life is increased by involvement and commitment which has purpose. We accept our responsibility to create within our Company an environment which encourages individual initiative and responsibility directed towards the fulfilment of personal and Company goals. We do not believe in uniformity as an end in itself, for this mostly leads to mediocrity and stifles creativity and leadership.

As industrial society increases in complexity, we recognise that success and real progress become more dependent on our ability to foster PARTNERSHIP and TEAMWORK between all who have a stake in our Company; between our shareholders and employees and with our wider stakeholders – our bankers, our customers, our sister professions, our sub-contractors and suppliers, the unions with whom we work and governments both State and Australian. This Partnership and Teamwork acknowledges that the whole is made up of the skills and experiences of all, that all have both the right to recognition and the obligation to act responsibly for the benefit of the whole.

We believe that leadership is necessary to make achievement possible – to produce sound results, to encourage individual initiative and to build teamwork. The partnership which we therefore strive to create is a partnership where the skills of all are recognised though they are not the same, where responsibility is accepted by all but where some are required to accept greater responsibility, and where rewards reflect the contribution of each to the whole.

As to profit, it is essential to our survival and to the growth of opportunity for all of our stakeholders. We believe that motivation will be stimulated by personal fulfilment and financial incentive. We assert that financial incentive maintains for the Company and for us as individuals a substantial measure of freedom of choice in what we do with the rewards of our efforts; we believe it to be a far preferable system to others which use status and power as the focus for incentive.

The quality of our corporate life is to be measured against our goal of EXCELLENCE in:

- the products we market and the value we provide
- the performance we achieve in quality, in time, and in consistent profitability
- the satisfaction of our customers
- technological leadership and innovation
- the motivation and job satisfaction of our employees
- the development of our employees
- our relationships with our employees
- our relationships with unions
- our contribution to industry and society
- the way we manage change.

Imposed on this already complex set of relationships were the impacts of two sets of adversarial conditions – the contract with the customer administered by the leading consultant, and the power of the construction trade unions, which reached its zenith in Australia in the 1970s. As technology developed, the scope for complexity in design and the inter-relationship between specialist elements such as heating, cooling, energy and lighting, and communication systems also increased. The number of design changes during construction multiplied as a consequence, and the adversarial nature of the contract frequently put consultant against contractor, contractor against customer, and consultant against customer in deciding who would pay for the costs of changes and delays. Technology and mechanisation also brought critical pieces of construction equipment to the site, such as the tower crane and the man/materials hoist on multi-storey buildings. These made the physical tasks easier but concentrated the power to disrupt in fewer hands.

This brief sketch of the conditions prevailing hardly presents a model scene or environment which would increase the probability of excellence, quality or respect. In these circumstances, construction companies survived mostly by some form of autocratic leadership, domineering or paternalistic. The highly systematised and organised practices then advocated widely for managing business enterprises – built on various adaptations of planning, staffing, reporting and control – contained useful elements but were too mechanistic to survive in the varied fields of general construction. The only alternative to these was to find a better way of working together. I had become convinced by that time that genuine teamwork was not only an option for Baulderstone, but that is was *the* option with the best long-term potential for the company and its people.

Beyond that, because of the frustrating diversions that flowed from the adversarial relationships and obligations imposed on the parties by the traditional form of contract, my colleagues and I became increasingly persuaded that teamwork between customer, design consultants and contractor would enhance the results and benefits to all parties. There was much scepticism and resistance in the market place at that time to this idea, which required treating the contractor as an equal amongst professionals – all contractors were rogues! But we persisted and in 1977 one government client agreed to give it a try. Thereafter, this partnership approach to project execution became a core service in the business and yielded large dividends for the vision and the investment.

The themes of leadership, partnership and profit were buttresses against what we saw as unworkable sectional political pressures and trends. Widespread conflict between employers and trade unions had become almost a trademark of Australian post-war industry and a severe barrier to improving productivity, competitiveness and reliability. Though South Australia was less affected than the more populous centres, conflict was on the increase and the reforming socialist State Government strongly promoted 'worker participation in management' as a solution. Visits to various parts of Europe, notably Sweden and Yugoslavia, were the sources of this movement and, in the mid-1970s, it seemed likely that the government would attempt to consolidate its objective through legislation to make 'worker participation' mandatory.

It was claimed that this approach would bring harmony, cooperation and increased productivity. It would result in 'teamwork' through its prescribed representative committees of workers, which would participate in and review management decisions. In some quarters, it was openly viewed as moving towards worker control. An adjunct to this thinking was the appointment of worker representatives to boards of directors, an idea which became fashionable for a time but gradually fell out of favour.

The essence of the 'worker participation' concept was, however, a contradiction. It claimed increased cooperation and productivity as its objective whereas its primary motivation and focus were power and influence in the enterprise – improvement in performance was only a secondary goal. We had learnt enough from our own study, experimentation and training to know that however well-intended, it was a charlatan which couldn't and wouldn't work. It would suffocate any genuine teamwork and was therefore a challenge to the roots of our own company-building.

Our philosophy would make it clear to ourselves as the executive team first, and progressively to our employees, that genuine teamwork had to be built on conviction and worked at consistently, and would require strong leadership which believed in fostering participation, encouraging initiative and making it possible to use diverse talents effectively and develop new ones.

Along with the political focus on increasing worker involvement and influence, 'profitability' – popularly perceived to be an exclusive reward of owners and bosses – became almost a dirty word in much public comment and debate. Anti-business sentiment is in any case not uncommon in Australian society, but the fanning of this dissent in the 1970s had more disturbing potential. For Baulderstone, still recovering from its near disaster in 1972, and with no other source of development funding except the reinvestment of earnings, profitability was the life blood of growth and development of the business and of the security of employment for everyone. It was important to make this fact explicit.

Chapter 9

LEADERSHIP AND
THE BOTTOM STEP

Barriers to growing

Common wisdom says to us that 'in every successful organisation leadership starts at the top'. This truism limits horizons of participation because it so often implies that leadership stays at the top and the organisation is sharply divided between the leaders and the led, between those who decide what to do and those who only do what they are told. This was, in fact, the real state of Baulderstone in the late 1950s and a core reason why Bert's business was vulnerable. Vulnerability of this kind presents a serious and difficult hurdle for the founder of almost every small business which grows.

There were other hurdles for Baulderstone. By the early 1980s the company was recognised as a very successful middle-sized Australian construction business which was knocking at the door of major national construction projects within its range of technical competence. It was financially strong for its size, with high liquidity and low debt, but because of its history had a smaller capital base relative to those enterprises categorised as major national contractors. The hurdle between it and major projects could be described as the aspiring smaller contractors' 'glass ceiling', with competitors, banks and owners manning the barricades.

Major construction projects usually require contractors to provide very large financial performance guarantees as a precondition of participation. We had recognised for at least a decade that there would almost certainly come a time when the reinvestment of earnings, constrained by the highly competitive nature of the Australian construction industry and the unsympathetic corporate tax system, would be insufficient to enable the company to break through this glass ceiling. There would come a time when some additional source of capital or financial backing would be necessary to permit further growth.

In 1983 our minds were not concentrated on this question; we were not thinking that this was the time for such an addition to the business. The expression of interest by a large international French construction group, Societe Auxiliaires d'Entreprises (SAE), came out of the blue – from the clear blue sky above the glass ceiling! We were sceptical, but thought that exploring the approach would be valuable experience. We found an unexpected compatibility and, in 1984, SAE acquired 20 per cent of Baulderstone, increasing its stake in future years. This new corporate partnership lasted ten years, and terminated when SAE lost its identity through a merger-acquisition brought about by its own weakness. Corporate survival can never be taken for granted.

The cause of SAE's weakness brings us back to the proposition that leadership stays at the top. SAE was one of the leading construction groups in France. Its record of strong continuous growth since the end of the Second World War had been fed firstly by the demand for post-war reconstruction in Europe and then by its ground floor participation in the Middle-Eastern construction boom following the oil crisis in 1973. By the end of that decade, growth in both markets was in decline. Anticipating these conditions, SAE initiated moves to establish itself in the United States and then in south-east Asia.

By the time SAE approached us in 1983, it had already acquired three businesses in the USA, each roughly the same size as Baulderstone, and was examining a fourth. The four were located strategically to cover progressively the widespread geography of the country. The existence of these American subsidiaries, which had several years of experience with their new shareholder – and spoke English – was a bonus for us in our study of SAE's interest in Baulderstone. All the conversations we had with their representatives on our study tour were positive about the new relationship and its potential.

This experience was confirmed in our discussions with SAE executives in France, with whom we found this unexpected compatibility. Louis, who was the director given responsibility for the new Australian member of the SAE family, was a marvellous person who by his integrity, openness and interest in everything Baulderstone was doing, and in its people, earned the respect and warm regard of many Baulderstone staff. He became a good friend.

International partnership – universal lessons

One impression of our study visit to the United States remained with me and increased as I had opportunity over the following years to meet more of the staff of SAE's American subsidiaries. To differing degrees, all the subsidiaries had limiting characteristics similar to Baulderstone in the late 1950s. In Baulderstone, these characteristics had remained latent and largely uncorrected during the 1960s and nearly brought disaster in 1972. Painful personal learning had heightened my awareness to these conditions.

The American businesses had been developed and driven by founders who were approaching retirement. Retirement is a particularly high hurdle for the business founder who is still owner when he wants to quit. SAE's desire to acquire had come like a double gift. Founders would receive financial rewards for all the labour of their years, while the businesses in which they had invested so much of themselves would continue. And so it was.

Each of these enterprises had an excellent track record and reputation. In that respect SAE had done its homework and chosen well. But leadership had stayed at the top. SAE's error of judgement was not to recognise the impact of the withdrawal of the founder's influence, and then to compound that weakness by promptly promoting rapid growth on the strength of the increased financial backing it was able to bring. When the problem was recognised it was too late. The projects in hand had the momentum of a runaway train. By the time the train was brought under control, the size of the losses incurred in the United States had absorbed too much of the strength, vitality and profitability even of this highly respected international enterprise, and it lost the support of its principal shareholders.

No business however large, strong or apparently impregnable is free from this leadership principle. **The role of those persons who are the**

leaders of enterprises which last (ie continue to grow in size, strength, diversity, and adaptability) **is to create the conditions for leadership development which will yield candidates for succession at all levels.** These conditions welcome and cultivate initiative in every part of the business, and make it possible for an employee to exercise leadership right where he or she is in the organisation.

This is what responsible and effective delegation demands. Delegation is an invitation to participate in leadership. Commitment to such participation and strength of identity with an enterprise increase when employees are invited to understand and share the enterprise's reason for being. To invite such a sharing is an act of respect to those invited. I think of it as the bottom step in long-term enterprise building.

The bottom step

Looking back in 1988 at what we had learned, I wrote to our employees:

> A statement of our reason for being gives purpose, direction and identity to our collective endeavours. Without purpose and direction, leadership is aimless and cannot be called leadership at all. At Baulderstone that statement is contained in our Group Philosophy – Towards Excellence.
>
> Philosophy is practical because it makes us face reality. Philosophy gives us roots; it therefore brings us down to earth so that we might reach towards the stars!
>
> You will have discovered yourselves that the person who is of greatest practical assistance in difficult times is frequently the person who has a clear, and generally simple, philosophy of life.
>
> Philosophy describes a set of stable values, attitudes and beliefs which provide direction for long-term development. This stability brings an underlying security to our thinking and planning which permits adaptation to changing situations and circumstances without being blown off course by every wind of change, be it social or economic in origin.
>
> Such a statement also enables us to take, on occasions, a pragmatic, less-than-desirable decision on a particular issue or in

relation to particular pressures if no better solution can be found (the construction industry is hardly free from such situations), but it prevents that decision from automatically lowering company standards by stealth, and acts as a barrier to the growth of ad-hocery.

Our corporate philosophy is not a statement saying 'we have arrived!' For this reason, to nail the colours of our broader aspirations and goals to the mast, as it were, is to expose ourselves and the Group to the risk of criticism where practice may be perceived to fall short of stated philosophy. The alternative, however, seems to me much worse – to accept the inevitability of a creeping mediocrity.

Our philosophy stands therefore as the prerequisite for leadership.

The words above were addressed to the employees of Baulderstone Hornibrook, not Baulderstone. Out of necessity, and with the motivation of harsh experience, Baulderstone worked hard after 1972 at building depth in leadership. It was therefore equipped to take advantage of the new backing brought by SAE's opportune involvement when the construction operations of Hornibrook came unexpectedly on the market in 1985. Hornibrook was older and had been in business longer than Baulderstone and had been the leading engineering construction company in Australia through the 1950s and 1960s. Unsupportive ownership change and its impact on leadership had diminished that status so that, by 1985, it was of similar size to Baulderstone. Its operations were complementary geographically and in engineering experience. Acquisition presented an opportunity to take that quantum leap in size, substance and recognition which would open up the market of very large projects, where the scope for improving financial returns by creative solutions was seen as greater.

Once the acquisition was made, the new business*, was immediately twice as large in volume, people and regions of operation. And

---

* Only the Company name Baulderstone is used in the continuing text and therefore means Baulderstone Hornibrook after 1985.

even though most of the leadership would have to come from Baulderstone, the business now had two cultures. Attempting to put into practice what had been learned from experience, we did not forget to include the bottom step.

Acquisition – the bottom step revisited

The Baulderstone Philosophy was written in 1975, and then issued and explained to managers in 1976 and to staff employees* in 1978. It was not made readily available to all employees until it had been redrafted in 1986. I had become cautious in trying to attempt too much too quickly – fearful of again creating misunderstanding and expectations that remained unfulfilled. Perhaps I was too cautious, but I wanted first to be confident that a high level of understanding and a sufficient level of commitment permeated the middle levels of responsibility.

The Hornibrook acquisition provided the opportunity as well as the necessity to revisit that task, to introduce former Hornibrook staff to Baulderstone purpose and values and to strengthen the ownership of these amongst all Baulderstone staff.

The philosophy was redrafted by the executive team to take account of the experience gained in the decade since it was first written. The objective was to make it more focused and concise without changing its essence. This time round, middle managers would participate in its finalisation through circulation of the draft and discussion in each region of operation with the chief executive.

Participation was genuine even though not many changes were made. I recall two particular experiences. The first eleven words, which had been part of the original statement but omitted in the redraft, were reincluded. An industrial relations manager convinced his colleagues of their importance when he explained that they had been a determining factor in his decision to join the company. He believed

---

* For reasons of clarity, it is necessary to distinguish between staff and employees in the rest of the text. 'Employees' means all employees of the enterprise or employees generally. 'Staff' refers to employees other than strongly unionised on-site employees, but usually includes union members who were leading hands or had long service with the company. The strength of construction trade unions referred to earlier was a significant barrier to the ways in which all employees could be included in enterprise-building activities and only began to change in the early 1990s.

BAULDERSTONE HORNIBROOK

Towards Excellence – Our Group Philosophy

(Revised statement, 1985)

Baulderstone Hornibrook exists for those who have a stake in it and, in return, these stakeholders have a community of interest which supports the continuity of the Group.

Because we intend therefore to be in business over the long term, we are committed to the development of distinctive capabilities and professional competence so that our customers receive the best value for service in the market.

Our aim is to be known for outstanding physical and financial performance, for the quality of our people and for the strength and creativity of our relationships with customers, employees, shareholders and associated enterprises and authorities.

Our corporate philosophy, expressed below, provides a structure of values and beliefs that enables us to accept the challenge of moving towards this strategic goal.

- We believe in leadership that builds partnership and teamwork and that the effort required to create the skills and conditions to sustain this kind of participation is worthwhile.
- We strive to create conditions in which every employee is challenged and encouraged to excel, where personal goals can be matched with the goals of the business, and where we all accept responsibility for the property and reputation of the Group.
- We acknowledge that excellence has the dimension of wholeness and that the pursuit of excellence brings obligations to recognise the interests of all who have a stake in the business, to act fairly, to practise integrity so that people can trust what we say, and to be a responsible member of society.
- Finally, arrogance has no place in the pursuit of excellence, whereas legitimate pride in achievement and genuine humility support it. We accept the challenge as worthy though the goal remains beyond our reach even as we make progress towards it. This reminds us that we never know it all and learn from every experience.

these words expressed a distinctive characteristic. The pursuit of conciseness in this case had been a false economy.

There were spirited debates in several regions about the word 'humility' in the last paragraph. The majority of middle managers were project staff. Their discomfort with this word and their challenge to its inclusion sprang from their equating humility with timidness, weakness and self-effacement – which they found hard to reconcile with the rough and tumble of the construction site. This discussion provided the opportunity to explore other possibilities and lead those who had expressed concern to an expanded understanding: humility is a quality of great strength and it is not possible to learn from experience without it. So humility was kept, while the challenge that had been made illustrated that whatever is written is never sufficient in itself without the continued effort to foster understanding.

An appraisal

Involving the company's middle managers in this way had been a time-consuming activity amongst all the other demanding tasks of building one integrated business from two. Was it worth it? Was it a legitimate priority?

The answers to these questions must in large part be subjective and anecdotal. Yet the following evidence points to the fruitfulness of being open about purpose and values to the whole organisation.

- Roots were deepened and deep roots were not unimportant in surviving the gale force winds which blew through the property and construction industries on all continents in the decade from 1985 to 1995, uprooting many enterprises.
- Over this decade, Baulderstone increased its market share, in a market which shrank in size, from $180 million immediately after acquiring Hornibrook to more than $800 million in 1995. Its profits were modest but it never posted a loss year in that period.
- A new level of ownership of the Group Philosophy was recognisable. The Queensland leadership took the initiative to frame and display it in every project and division office so that it could

be used as a constant reminder of purpose and a standard for critique of the company's direction and daily operations. The rest of the organisation soon followed Queensland's example.

- At the time of this writing, the Group Philosophy has not changed. In 1989 the executive team strengthened its commitment by including in the policy statement of its own role the specific obligation for 'promoting and expressing through example and action the vision, philosophy and values of the Group'.

- Baulderstone retained its Australian identity and leadership through ten years of ownership and partnership with SAE, its identity surviving beyond that of its owner shareholder. The relationships of mutual respect and cooperation that had been forged between the executives of SAE and Baulderstone were stronger than the difficulties through which SAE was passing. When the decision was made by SAE that it no longer wished to maintain an Australian operation, the task of finding a new owner was undertaken jointly. The resulting transfer of ownership was achieved to the benefit of both. Despite the unsympathetic market, SAE was well rewarded for its ten-year investment in Baulderstone, and Baulderstone gained a new principal with greater financial strength, a keen interest in expanding in Asia and sufficient compatibility on which to keep on building the future.

This evidence is not intended to claim that being open about purpose produced these outcomes single-handedly or that it was all pervasive. Rather, it enabled a sufficiently firm foundation to be laid to support all the actions that collectively contributed to the results achieved.

Part 3

LEADERSHIP AND PARTICIPATION

Openness about Direction

*We believe in leadership that builds partnership
and teamwork and that the effort required to create
the skills and conditions to sustain this kind of
participation is worthwhile.*

Chapter 10

WE BELIEVE IN LEADERSHIP ... SOMETIMES

Fashion and leadership

During the last 40 years or so people have watched language change in many spheres of life. In literature describing roles in organisational life, 'boss' and 'subordinate' have become 'manager' and 'staff' – have become 'team leader' and 'team member', have become 'facilitator' and 'participant', have become ... When the emphasis changed to 'the inspirer' and 'the inspired', there was a degree of coming full circle by another name! Unfortunately, leadership without perspiration loses its inspiration.

Language does not change the reality. Frequent changes in terms can indicate a problem to be addressed or an opportunity to be realised. In this case, the change in terms initially accompanied a search for ways of achieving better results for the enterprise by breaking down the constricting authority and control of rigid hierarchy in order to enhance both the effectiveness and the satisfaction of its people. Later came others who saw language more as a tool for social engineering than the crafting of description, understanding and communication. The authority of leaders wasn't really necessary. Everyone's contribution counts equally, surely? It is the temptation of an assertion which is both true and not true.

How organisations function is not changed by changing the terms we use. There are very few enterprises or groups which can operate satisfactorily without any hierarchy of responsibilities and the authority that underpins responsibility. Where it is tried, the resulting confusion becomes an invitation to a new round of dictatorial direction. This is one thing which happened in the 1980s in the wake of the rise of focus on individuality through the previous two decades. Many attempts by organisations to involve their people more, particularly through the use of prescribed consultation and committees, had produced the opposite result to that intended – performance was inhibited and bureaucracy increased. So corporate heads who operated much like dictators emerged in the 1980s to 'cut through the crap'. Short-term results improved, often dramatically, and they were much praised while they were successful. But by the end of the decade many of them were being condemned. What is important, and what can vary widely, is not the existence of hierarchy but how it is used. In 1975 we stated explicitly in the Baulderstone Philosophy that 'we believe in leadership'. Making a clear distinction with prevailing fashion was not the only influence; there was a more pressing reason why these words were retained in the re-write in 1985. We had experienced the severe pain and distress caused by the abdication of leadership, one of the most common failings of leaders everywhere. It comes clothed in many different disguises.

So having opted *for* leadership, for what were we striving? Were there viable alternatives to the extremes of a kind of dictatorship on the one hand and some form of sentimentalised involvement on the other. We wrestled with the question: is there a legitimate (in the sense of mutually beneficial) relationship between leaders and the way they exercise leadership in an enterprise which espouses respect for its people as a core value but still has to perform in the market place? between the responsibility the leader bears for the enterprise, and the responsibility he or she bears for its people individually and collectively? I found these hard questions, hard lessons to learn. I now believe an authentic response lies in facing up to the twin disciplines of *competence* and *compassion* in all decision making. These disciplines force the decision-maker to look beyond the hard-nosed solution, the soft option and the status quo. Facing up to the demands and consequences of both competence and compassion is an essential mark of leadership which seriously aims to achieve openness about direction.

Abdication – lesson one

Building breadth of competence is one of the most demanding challenges faced by a growing enterprise, and particularly by every small enterprise which chooses to grow beyond the capacity of its founder to control it. Baulderstone stumbled, almost faltering, over this challenge three times.

The circumstances in each case are instructive. The first, already described in chapter six, occurred when Bert appointed his first manager, promoted him beyond his level of knowledge and experience and then failed to provide reasonable support or direction. He abdicated his leadership responsibility in both ways. It is almost a textbook illustration of the risky consequences of a critical decision taken in desperation (in this case Bert's growing anxiety about his health). The distractions created by circumstances which make decision-makers overly anxious provide the justifications for decisions which lack rigour and objectivity.

However, as a wise humorist once remarked, 'success is the ability to survive failure', a prediction made probable when the crisis survived leads to facing up and learning. The company in those years of the late 1950s had clearly been operating beyond its real level of competence. It had many good and loyal employees but almost no control systems and no employees who could become leaders.

Abdication – lesson two

A determined effort was made to face up to and correct this imbalance in the first half of the 1960s, so that by 1965 Baulderstone was beginning to be recognised as a local industry leader in its use of the latest construction equipment and methods, its application of critical path planning to estimating and projects, and its computerised cost-control system. Basic training had been introduced for supervisors and foremen to improve their skills in work planning, supervision and control, and to gain their involvement in, and contribution to, the changes being made.

The second half of the 1960s therefore commenced on a strong note of success in construction achievement, a return to improved and consistent profitability and rejuvenated morale. Civil engineering construction had become well established as a new sphere of activity, while good fortune in winning successive large contracts as part of the complete rebuilding of Adelaide's major hospital helped propel the company into a significant new growth phase in the years 1965 to 1968, all within South Australia and the regular oversight of head office. There was even time to start thinking about the future!

These were good years. They drew a veil over the traumas and vulnerability of 1960 and softened the hard, sharp edges of Bert's earlier learning, in which I had hardly shared given my newness to the company and my inexperience.

Beware the good times for they will surely pass. Clouds were already forming to create stormy weather. The company would again almost founder. Baulderstone was on the brink of its second crisis of competence.

The market place was changing dramatically. In the space of two or three years in the mid-1960s at least four national construction companies established operations in the relatively small South Australian market, more than doubling Baulderstone's immediate competition. All had more financial strength and experienced people than Baulderstone.

Management development was progressing too slowly at Baulderstone. Some steps had been taken to select employees with potential and equip them to share the leadership in the functions of estimating, contract administration, project management, accounting and training. A considerable investment in relation to the company's size had been made by providing the opportunity for several of these managers to attend a ten-day residential executive staff course which I had found stimulating and useful in 1961, but the benefits were less than hoped for.

Some recruitment had been tried with limited success. Experienced construction staff with executive potential were not much interested in a medium-sized company with its operations still limited to the modest State market. At the same time, I had a heavy bias towards encouraging the development of our own people who had demonstrated their loyalty. The hard reality therefore was that in 1968, with Bert less and less involved, there was only one other manager, also by then a director, who was able to be a genuine colleague to me in the task of developing and leading the business.

Thrown in at the deep end as general manager in 1963, one fundamental business lesson I learned very early was the critical importance of cash. Though the company had survived in 1960, the constant pressure from creditors for payment was to continue until 1965 before improved performance restored an adequate cash flow. I hated the stress from this kind of pressure to pay and vowed not to allow it to happen again. It was a somewhat empty vow made without the authority to fulfil it.

Peter Donovan records what happened next:

> For all its apparent success and increased professionalism, the Company in the late 1960s lost its clear sense of direction as Bert confused what he wanted and liked to do with what he should have done. It was a time when Bert justifiably sought to enjoy the benefits of his achievements. Yet by using the resources of the Company in primarily personal endeavours, he compromised the sense of purpose which had marked it to that time.
>
> ... Bert Baulderstone was a single-minded individual, who invited participation in discussion but generally did things in his own way. Because of his business acumen this had served him and the Company well, until the mid-to-late 1960s ... Bob Mierisch recalls that the only serious disagreement that he ever had with Bert was over the latter's wish to diversify into primary production. It was Mierisch's concern that after the problems of the credit squeeze in the early 1960s and the hard work to re-establish the Company's liquidity, the results of this effort should not be lost, and that it was also a strange move to diversify into an area in which the Company had no evident expertise.

During 1966 and 1967 the company outlaid close to $200,000 on these ventures, absorbing a major part of its liquidity. At about the same time the business cycle turned and the market headed towards recession at the close of the decade.

In the face of these gathering storm clouds (intensified local competition, declining market, reduced cash and stretched business leadership), I made two decisions, presented them in the form of strong recommendations to the board and gained the board's support. One decision was sound, the other was not.

The sound decision was to seek external help to set up the sustained internal staff training and development program which had been our desire and good intention for five years. While we had made a start, perhaps several starts, our good intentions had failed to deliver because my efforts in particular, and those of some helpers, were being constantly diverted to other immediately pressing priorities such as winning enough work to keep the business operating and our people employed so as not to allow our recently improved expertise to be dissipated.

The unsound decision was to seek to win some of that needed new work in remote (3000 kilometres remote) greener pastures, the booming centre of Dampier, development site for Western Australia's huge iron ore discoveries. After tendering unsuccessfully for a number of contracts over the best part of a year, during which time the company's forward work orders continued to shrink, we won a small contract in Dampier in 1968. I recall, and often regret that I did not keep as a salutary reminder, a copy of the letter I wrote to all our staff announcing this small contract, certain to be the first of many, and informing them how the work was to be managed. Its enthusiastic tone would expose, in retrospect, my blinkered intention to see the opportunity 'writ large' while masking my unwillingness to face up to the risks arising from our inexperience and the potential impact of this demanding move on our systems and depleted financial resources.

In a way history was about to repeat itself, for there was an element of desperation in looking for work so far away as part of our response to the sudden deterioration of the home market. However, what I call 'creeping justification' was the most serious characteristic of the abdication of leadership which led to this second brush with extinction.

The company set aside my director colleague and our most experienced project manager to guide this new venture, competent leadership well beyond what was needed for the first small contract, but necessary with our eyes on the future. We had the first step right. When we were not successful in obtaining immediate follow-up work in Dampier, partly due to an unanticipated drop in the work available, we made the decision to open a branch office in Perth, 2000 kilometres from Adelaide and 1500 kilometres from Dampier. We had learned from our initial experience in Dampier that a base in Perth would be necessary in order to be more competitive in winning and servicing work in the iron ore region; it would also give us, we rationalised, access to the bustling Perth market as a further option.

Our two senior officers agreed to move to Perth in 1969 to establish the new branch office. When they both had to return to Adelaide for personal reasons after 12 months, the company had won some work in Perth while continuing to bid for the reduced opportunities in Dampier. Although our director manager retained responsibility for this operation, the moves meant that all the activity in Western Australia would be under the direct control of the largely untested staff recruited during the previous year.

With regard to the work opportunities in Dampier, we had behaved rather like the donkey tempted by the carrot. We had missed the first wave of development and the next stage proved continually to be just around the corner – a successful ploy by the customer to retain our involvement in its interests of preserving competition. When the work didn't come, we should have faced up to the changed conditions and withdrawn in spite of the disappointment. Instead we hung on, increasing the company's vulnerability by adding a Perth office and work in Perth which was not part of the original decision, and then exposing the company to real risk by not replacing proven officers to provide direct control early in 1970.

The Western Australian market was by then entering its own downward cycle, but not even this daunted our optimism. We *could* and *would* be successful – five new contracts at Dampier, won in June 1971, fed that confidence. Three months later the first cracks began to appear, but it took another six months to diagnose the magnitude of the problem, the extent of projected losses and the threat to the company. Not only our people, but also our systems, had been shown to be inadequate for the control of contracts so remote from the company's centre.

Circumstances finally forced on us the decision we had refused to make voluntarily – to withdraw from Western Australia. It came after three years of creeping justification. This is not an uncommon experience in business and life. **When an important decision that needs to be made is avoided, events will sooner or later make that decision for us, but at a time when the conditions and impact are almost always less favourable than when it was first avoided.** In Baulderstone's case, sorting out the mess and winding up the operations in Dampier and Perth became my personal task because the company's survival was at stake. It was a case of the punishment fitting the crime!

The biggest part of the task, with the greatest ongoing risks to the company, was the completion of contracts in Dampier. I will never forget the experience of the first two days when I sat in the hot, dusty site office ten kilometres east of Dampier near the end of summer in 1972, studying the reports and progress statements of the incomplete contracts. It took only those two days to understand that we had spent two-thirds of the money and done less than one-third of the work. Clearly the worst of the financial stresses were yet to come. To observe the way the project staff worked and thought was to understand part of the reason why. I had to admit to myself that neither the staff responsible in the Perth office, nor my former director colleague had been able, or willing, to see the problem in spite of regular site visits. It left an indelible impression. Nothing can be done successfully without the necessary discipline and competence.

The company survived its second crisis because its South Australian operation had remained strong, because my immediate management colleagues gave their wholehearted support, and thanks to the unstinting efforts of a core group of our best and most loyal construction staff who moved from Adelaide to Dampier and shared the task of finishing the troublesome contracts.

In contrast with this saga, the sound decision of four years earlier had yielded returns. The wholehearted support of my colleagues had come, in part, from strengthened cohesion, communication and cooperation in the South Australian management team to a level which permitted my, and the core group's, extended absence in Western Australia, without detriment to the company's other operations.

Another consequence of the initial steps that had been taken in staff and organisation development had forced the company, for the first time, to face up to the absence of real financial expertise within its ranks. While this deficiency had been recognised for a number of years, we needed the support and confidence of external advice based on a wider business experience to act with the urgency and seriousness necessary. As a result we had been able to recruit a young finance director of exceptional ability in February 1971. His hands-on support, given without reservation, in finalising the company's affairs in Western Australia made a crucial contribution to survival. My gratitude left me wondering why so new a recruit had stayed with so much at stake. Much later, he told me that he stayed partly because he recognised the extraordinary experience he was gaining!

The financial problems stretched further, in fact, than just Western Australia, for right in the midst of these demands Bert died suddenly and unexpectedly in March 1972. His family home and his farms comprised a very substantial part of the company's assets.

Our new finance director soon uncovered why our systems had not given more warning signs of the pending losses in Western Australia. The site-related cost controls and company-related accounting functions were not progressively integrated or reconciled. Though the company had employed professional accountants for years, none had really understood the business. There was therefore a serious gap in their ability to contribute as leaders. During the 1960s my direct involvement in and detailed knowledge of the structure of our tenders, of methods, costs and potential margins, and my close contact with projects during their execution because they were near enough to home base, had given me sufficient feel for our operating performance to know that the business was sound and to make sure that forecasts were conservative. By this means, we had been able to create reserves and enhance liquidity. The lack of effective reconciliation between cost control and accounting systems was, therefore, not exposed – not until the tyranny of distance imposed the necessity of sound systems.

It is easy to miss the emerging patterns of repetition when you are closely and continuously involved. Bert had managed his business virtually without formal systems, primarily using his 'little black book', in which he kept his observations and productivity records, and the cheque book and bank balance. When he withdrew his involvement, the business faltered. We had developed much more comprehensive control processes in the ten years since those events, but when growth and distance made it no longer possible for me to retain detailed involvement in all tenders and projects, critical limitations in our systems and our people were exposed and the business faltered again. If it was true that the company had been operating beyond its level of real competence at the end of the 1950s, it was true also at another level at the end of the 1960s.

Abdication – lesson three

Abdication of leadership is a frailty that can always sneak upon us when we are distracted. I had observed the consequences of Bert's abdication through the justification of desperation. I had nearly lost the business and endured the personal stresses of my and the board's abdication through the creeping justification of continuing to support an unsound decision by seeing only opportunities and seeing these through rose-tinted glasses. But ten years later I fell into the trap again, abdicating leadership through the weakness of self-indulgence.

As it had done following survival from its first crisis in the early 1960s, the company set about learning from its hard years of experience in the early 1970s. Out of the ruins of the Western Australian venture, the foundations for its long-term future were firmly laid. As the company gathered itself together over the next year, building on the successful recruitment of its new finance director, it attracted two further directors, responsible for marketing and construction, with special skills and proven track records in large and complex construction contracts. A little later a third executive was recruited, a specialist in Australian industrial relations. I now had four peer-level colleagues with whom to share the building of the company. For a few years it would appear to some that the company was now top heavy for the scope of its operations, an overkill of competence perhaps. But this was not so, for there was much company-building to be done. The investment started to yield excellent dividends within three years.

My third dramatic lesson in the dangers of abdicating leadership came in the normal course of operations. The company was successful and had been growing strongly. The industry had entered its next period of recession – it is widely acknowledged that the business cycle in the construction industry is amongst the most pronounced and volatile of all industries. Downturns in the cycle almost always create pressures on work continuity, market volume and hard won skills, equipment, experience and enthusiasm. We were experiencing these pressures, particularly in our engineering operations.

As a result, I had been under constant pressure for a number of months from our marketing director to give approval to bid for work in northern Australia. He had already made a very valuable contribution to the company's development and expanded range of activities through his talent for creating new customers and opportunities. For a year he had diligently devoted time and energy to fostering opportunities to participate in a major new mining development in the north. Remote and mining, again! I had resisted his latest recommendation, as well as the temptation to support him in this particular contract opportunity, because the timing had not worked out and I did not believe we had the right people available. Even though we had a fleet of suitable equipment coming free from another site, a considered strategic decision had been made shortly before to establish operations in Sydney, Australia's largest city and capital of its most populous State. This was a priority.

But the pressure from my enthusiastic and determined colleague increased. Detailed bids were prepared, evaluated and recommended for final approval. In the end, I relented with these words to the marketing director: 'I'll support your recommendation, but if we have a problem, you will fix it!'

It was almost total abdication. I had caved in to the self-indulgence of not wishing to be seen as rigidly unreasonable, as a suppressor of initiative, opportunity, effort and enthusiasm. I knew that if we had a problem, he couldn't fix it. He was not competent in that way. His very considerable talents lay in other areas. We did have a problem! And I had to fix it, because the company was at risk again – this time, from the withholding of moneys which we considered legitimately due as a result of changes, delays and additions to the work emanating from our clients. Though the company's liquidity was by then strong for its size, withholding three million dollars absorbed most of it. We did eventually get all our money, but it took six months of full-time personal effort, and many grey hairs.

Facing up to difficult choices

These three experiences of leadership abdication illustrate the dilemma of facing up to what is real and making difficult choices. Very often the choice is subject to the competing pulls of competence and compassion, the word I chose to convey genuine concern and consideration for employees when decisions affecting them need to be made. This dilemma arises constantly in every enterprise, testing the enterprise's credibility.

Consider issues surrounding promotion, recruitment and continuity of employment. Respect for its people requires an enterprise to foster initiative, an essential element of leadership, in order to improve performance in every position. Competence demonstrated leads to aspirations and opportunities for promotion. I hold the belief strongly that every person has latent capacities which can be tapped and then grow to enrich life and work. Over the years I watched this happen in Baulderstone many times. I therefore had a strong desire to encourage and support the development of our people to do their jobs better and to prepare them for promotion. This desire was sometimes also accentuated by necessity. I wanted the company to grow and in the 1960s our attempts at recruitment rarely identified outsiders more competent than our internal candidates.

When signs began to show that a person promoted or recruited was not performing satisfactorily in the position, I too frequently persisted for too long in trying to make the appointment, ie the earlier decision, work. In so doing, I sacrificed the demand for high standards of competence to what I saw as my responsibility to the employee for my part in making the appointment. I had to learn two seemingly self-evident lessons; or, rather, to learn to practise them.

The first was that competence, the measure of knowledge, experience and application required in any position, must be congruent with the degree of responsibility that the position holds towards the whole enterprise and its stakeholders (responsibility here means the ability to influence or impact on the welfare of the whole enterprise through opportunity or risk). I failed to discern the significance of this requirement or face up to its hard-edged discipline in growing the company during the 1960s. It is true that there were barriers at that time to recruiting people with the levels of competence seen in retrospect as necessary, while inexperience was also a factor. However, if I had understood clearly what was needed and faced up to the possible consequences of proceeding with less than that, I would also have understood the high risk exposure and been better equipped to manage it.

The second lesson was to recognise and accept in every individual situation the difference between genuine concern and the temptation towards self-indulgence. If, after reasonable opportunity and appropriate support, an employee, whether leading hand or executive, is not showing the competence needed in the position held, it is rarely ever in the genuine interests of that employee to let him or her stay in it, no matter how much he or she wants to or how great their disappointment. Beyond this, accepting partial competence in one position challenges the credibility of an enterprise's declared commitment to high quality and excellence and is a demotivating influence on others. Selective self-indulgence cannot be fenced off for the enterprise or the employee.

To give one example, a pay officer had worked for the company for more than 20 years. When the subsidiary office where he had started was closed, he was transferred to a position in head office. He was a second-generation employee whose father had been Bert's first truck driver. He was loyal and diligent but, as the nature of his job changed, he seemed to fit in less and less. It took several years for the company to face up to this growing difficulty: how would it be seen in its dealings with this loyal and long-serving employee? When it finally did, the employee left and bought a small newsagency, after which life for him just blossomed.

Redundancy is another increasingly common situation. Over the 20 years from 1960, changes in the way work was executed in commercial and engineering construction forced the company to discontinue the operations of almost all the trade subsidiaries Bert had set up. In each case, cessation involved transfers, redundancies and support to place employees with other employers. These difficulties were mostly managed in ways which preserved mutual respect and dignity because we had learned to put our cards on the table.

A final word on the subject of this chapter comes from a mentor friend who said of this challenge to leadership: 'The leader who is responsible must be ruthless in searching for and taking the right decision, but always generous in its implementation'. I gradually learned to move in this direction, but it was never easy. In this, I take some consolation from the thought that if the decisions ever do come easily, it might just mean that substance has been sacrificed for appearance.

Chapter 11

LEADERSHIP THAT BUILDS PARTNERSHIP AND TEAMWORK

What is teamwork?

The essence of leadership that builds partnership and teamwork is contained in the words *come* and *this way*. Each is inclusive, each expresses invitation ahead of direction.

The first requirement of leaders who choose to seek this end is to believe in participation and teamwork. Perhaps I'm stating the obvious. But when words become cheapened by over-use, it is sometimes necessary to restate the obvious. Believing in participation requires that, as well as expecting each employee to make a productive contribution, he or she is invited to share in the thinking of the organisation and the way in which his or her work is being executed. It is genuinely believed the employee's understanding and ideas are of value.

Something worthy of such strong convictions will be costly. This Baulderstone discovered by experience, and from that experience concluded that the effort required to create the skills and conditions to sustain this kind of participation is worthwhile. This experience challenges a more popular view which proclaims that 'everyone believes in teamwork'. Text books and management journals advocate it. Promotional literature and advertising of many enterprises declare that 'we have it!' **But the truth is that genuine teamwork is rare.**

Many managers would be amongst the most vocal critics should their favoured sporting team lose an important match because only half of the team turned out to training. Yet most of the same managers expect that effective teamwork will be present in their own enterprises and teams simply because they like the idea and have so decreed: 'We work as a team here.'

Consider the conditions for membership of a basketball team (or almost any ball-sports team) with premiership aspirations. In addition to knowing that they must possess the basic skills and aptitudes, members accept the disciplines of fitness, training, coaching, critique after the game and strategy and tactics for future games. Therefore, when the team is on the court, each member understands the game plan, each player's particular role, and the carefully practised individual plays between various members on which the winning strategy is based. The rewards for commitment, courage and contribution include the exhilaration of being part of a winning team, outstanding sporting achievement and, for some, financial reward and security.

Few enterprises, or departments within them, work at their team-building with the same dedication as is shown by the local sporting team, let alone the State side. The result? Much opportunity for improved productivity and performance goes begging. Another result is that, irrespective of what the manager says or of the manager's good intentions, the enterprise or department is likely to be managed in either an autocratic manner (closely directed by the manager in a strongly authoritarian or paternalistic way) or a bureaucratic manner (controlled by position, politics and systems).

It is possible that the same manager may achieve a measure of participation by involving people in committees or activities which build camaraderie through social or after hours contact. The conclusion to be drawn from these observations, therefore, is not that there is nothing of value in these ways of managing, but that they do not constitute genuine teamwork.

The lesson stands. Unless an enterprise works continuously and with strong commitment at developing and maintaining the skills and attitudes that make effective teamwork possible, the inevitable consequence is that it will be managed in ways better described as autocratic or bureaucratic. To repeat, the consequence is that much opportunity for improved productivity and performance will go begging. Baulderstone's experience showed that both short-term and long-term performance will suffer.

A manager concerned to build sound teamwork into operations will therefore direct his or her leadership abilities and priorities towards creating the conditions where direction in the team comes mostly from the following:

- shared goals
- clear objectives and plans
- agreed standards
- understanding and commitment to goals, objectives, plans and standards
- the team member who has the greatest knowledge and skill in a particular subject or activity exercises the greatest influence on decisions and actions related to that subject or activity
- self control
- systematic and spontaneous critique.

These are pre-conditions for genuine teamwork.* When these conditions are present, the manager needs to spend only a small proportion of time supervising and directing other team members. More of his or her time is spent producing, contributing directly to improving team results.

Every team trains

From the events described in chapter ten, it is clear that Baulderstone had not established the preceding conditions during the 1960s for reasons including lack of knowledge, inexperience and the pressing needs to improve basic practical and technical competence. Had we been able to do so, I am certain we would have avoided some of the errors and omissions that were made.

The years 1970–71 provide a contrast. It was because we had done enough work during these two years with the company's then senior management group to begin to rectify this situation that the finance

---

* From this point on in the text, except where chosen to give special emphasis, the adjectives genuine, effective, sound etc have not been used with the terms team and teamwork. 'Team' is used only for those work groups which are working hard to develop team skills so that their 'teamwork' is legitimately genuine teamwork.

director and I were able in 1972 to devote our single-minded attention to winding up the debacle in Western Australia.

When the company had assembled a new leadership team with a higher level of business experience, an opportunity of increased dimension was presented which would further test and validate the teamwork premises the company had by then embraced for its development as an entity. A mark of this team was the diversity of its members' contributions.

I have already sketched my background. The finance director grew up in England but had lived most of his adult life in New Zealand; he had qualifications in accounting and economics and had worked in the newspaper and shipping industries. The marketing director was an Australian civil engineer who had extensive experience in project design and contractor supervision in the mining, heavy manufacturing and food processing industries. The construction director was a Yorkshireman who studied quantity surveying while working on sites around the north of England; he had gained broad experience of life and construction on several continents, and was a penetrating judge of people and an outstanding negotiator. The director of industrial relations was a Scot who had been a master seaman and harbourmaster; he turned to industrial relations in shipping and ship construction and then became a specialist adviser to manufacturing industry. Our personalities were no less diverse than our experience.

We trained hard in our team-building, accepting the disciplines of structured learning as well as working together at strengthening and developing the company. We gained a deep respect for each other and a keen awareness of each other's strengths and limitations. Diversity created conflict which we had to learn both to confront and how to confront, sometimes with considerable difficulty and heart-searching. Diversity was also the source of real team creativity, building on one person's idea, sparking new ones, and producing better team solutions than any individual one. We learnt to weight contributions according to the issue under consideration and so practised the art of permitting leadership to come from the source of greatest competence in the team.

Experience in this team equipped us to encourage and coach other work teams in the application of the same disciplines. The figure on pages 74–5 presents one summary of the disciplines of teamwork. It was used widely in introducing our people to the basics of team-building.

Learning to work together

We learned the importance of articulating responsibilities and expectations clearly for each employee in the context of team action. When the analogy of the basketball team was used earlier, reference was made to 'the carefully practised individual plays between various members' which are so important to success. Responsibility statements rarely even acknowledge this dimension of team action which provides a substantial platform of opportunity for improving team results.

Every employee as a team member has four sets of responsibilities. It follows that every manager who is a team leader has eight because he is a member of two teams, his own and that of his boss.

The four sets are:

- individual responsibilities
- responsibilities to and with each team member
- responsibilities to and with several team members together
- responsibilities to and with the whole team.

Individual responsibilities describe the member's personal contribution to the team's goals in accordance with role and talents. It is the contribution that no-one else makes or can make. For the basketballer on the court, it expresses itself in individual play: running, passing, defending, shooting for goal. It also includes off-the-court activities: the effort put in to achieving a high standard of personal fitness so the player gives his or her best for the whole game. It is that quality of play which results from training and practice he or she does alone to sharpen reflexes, improve ball skills.

Similar individual obligations apply to the manager as to the member. The manager's job is not just, and not primarily, to allocate tasks and supervise the members of his or her team. These are part of the responsibilities, but only a small part. He or she must, for example, keep focus – through observation, measurement, evaluation and anticipation – on those elements of the team's task that are most critical to its ultimate success. The manager must do the thinking and preparation necessary to enable ideas and plans to be conveyed to other members of the team making it easy for them to contribute and critique.

Responsibilities to and with each team member cover the work which must be done between pairs in order to be done effectively. It can be likened to the plays between two basketball forwards or backs, how they combine to pass the ball, to get around or trap opponents. To develop these skills they talk and practise together. Much of the effective output in all group activities depends on these one-to-one relationships irrespective of whether the two persons work in the same location or not. Where there is teamwork, the one-to-one relationships between colleagues are just as important as those between each team member and the manager.

The third set of responsibilities occurs where several members of a team, but not the whole team, work together to achieve a particular part of the result. A classic sporting picture is the build-up across the field in a rugby team pressing for a try. These sub-teams also have to work at their teamwork.

Finally, there are some activities which require all team members to be together in the same place. In the basketball team, meeting to critique the last game and to understand strategy and tactics for the next is one example. Here the captain and the coach have particular responsibilities to make such meetings of the whole team happen and work. Individual members have responsibility to the whole team to be present, to contribute their own knowledge and perspective about past events and future plans, and to raise any issues, including those which may be sensitive or controversial, that they see as important to achieving the team's purpose. This analogy holds true for every work team that aspires to be a winning team. The whole-team-together activities are critical to generating an atmosphere of openness, enthusiasm and commitment. These are the times and places where every member receives the same information at the same time; contradictory information and positions can be confronted and resolved; barriers are built against the growth of politics and manipulation.

MUSTS FOR LEADERSHIP WHICH BUILDS STRONG TEAMWORK

Leadership and teamwork – training notes 1976

THE SIX MUSTS	EXPLANATORY NOTES	ACTIONS I MUST TAKE TO HAVE THEM IN MY JOB AND MY TEAM

1. **Know destination and direction.**	This is the first requirement of the team leader.	• Describe my destination in quantitative and qualitative terms that cover such requirements as productivity, customer needs, profit, cost, people, knowledge required.
		• Describe my direction taking note of critical signs and markers that indicate progress, dangers and opportunities, eg make the best use of:
		  – plans and milestones – watch for deviations.
		  – strengths of methods and team members.

2. **Allocate responsibility for end products.**	Many managers focus most attention on telling people what to do and how to do it. When, however, attention is focused on the result required, the responsibility of how that result is achieved can be delegated to others within their level of experience and competence.	• Write down in clear language what I must produce and achieve and what each member of my team must produce and achieve. • Discuss with each team member to ensure we both have the same understanding and expectations. • Have team members exchange these statements so that each understands what is required of other members.
3. **See that necessary tasks are done in the best way.**	Effective delegation does not mean reinventing the wheel, but requires us to make use of the best knowledge and experience available.	• Write down what I must do, when it must be done and to what standards. • Have written down (by me or my team member) what he or she must do – how, when, to what standards. Agree it. • Decide on how tasks will be started and how problems will be corrected and improvements made (instruction, coaching, advice, self learning against a plan). • Critique progress, experience and results in order to learn and make improvements.

THE SIX MUSTS	EXPLANATORY NOTES	ACTIONS I MUST TAKE TO HAVE THEM IN MY JOB AND MY TEAM
4. Determine priorities for normal action, problem solving, crises.	A key responsibility of the manager as team leader is to see and understand the whole task better than any other team member. Keeping the whole task in mind is essential to determining priorities.	• I, myself, must know the things that are essential and urgent, those that are important and those that are less urgent or optional, and what the differences are. • Keep the two or three actions that will most influence the result continuously in my mind. Update and review my thinking to take account of progress and external changes.
5. Include others in my thinking about the job in hand.	Team members are neither robots nor mind readers.	• Brief my team on the overall plan, bench marks, critical opportunities. Invite contribution. • Discuss specific, important items of today's experience formally and informally – to learn, to improve methods, to encourage. • Have team members prepare short-term plans. Encourage ideas, agree actions. If the member is inexperienced, do the initial planning for him or her and get agreement.
6. Treat others as people.	Treating others as people also includes these musts for motivation: • my own competence. • justice – my people know they will be treated fairly. • integrity – my words and actions are consistent and the same standards apply to myself and others. • my enthusiasm and confidence.	• The contribution of team members is important. They are important. • Know each other's expectations in the job and write these down if necessary for understanding and record. • Know my own strengths and weaknesses and those of others. • Know the goals and interests of those who work with me. • Introduce regular, frank two-way critique of performance and relationships in a way which works and is helpful.

If thinking about these inter-related sets of responsibilities seems unnecessarily complicated, it is not more complicated than the way things are. If any of them are ignored, dismissed or not recognised, problems in coordination, cohesion and cooperation will be created and the ability to capitalise on opportunities will be diminished. Collectively, results will be poorer. Therefore every enterprise which aspires to persistent high standards of performance must find ways to incorporate these requirements into their formal and informal processes. This task does not have to become swamped in words and paper. It is possible to be concise, centering on the substance. It is the understanding and acceptance of this network of relationships that is important, along with the enthusiasm for the increased possibilities which are released.

I write from experience more than theory. The pair and sub-team work units in the leadership team provided the driving force for most of the key tasks in project winning and execution at Baulderstone. Our willingness to work at strengthening these units as a separate element of team building lifted the effectiveness and influence of the whole team and was a primary contributor to the company's growth and success from 1975.

When open and creative relationships are encouraged, and in fact required as a condition of team membership, real benefits result to individual team members in terms of knowledge, learning and problem-solving support. These benefits flow through them to the whole enterprise. When an enterprise makes the time to cultivate these practices, a new freedom and openness begins to develop. People become less inhibited by hierarchy and can seek advice and support directly from anywhere in the enterprise within the limits of what is practical.

Cultivating and maintaining the conditions for teamwork takes commitment and effort. Sometimes it's a slog, mostly it's stimulating, sometimes it's fun. Always it is worth it.

Chapter 12

THE GAME PLAN

Competing priorities

Members of winning teams come together to study the last game in order to improve tactics and performance for future games. They understand the game plan.

In 1971 Baulderstone needed a game plan, or at least one that related to the league in which we aspired to play. Pressured in its own market place by larger, stronger competitors with more resources and knowledge at their disposal, and stretched thin by growth and geographical spread of which some was sound and some was not, the evidence for this need is plain to see – at least in retrospect.

But there were many pressing needs, as usually there are, some immediate, others longer term. They were inter-dependent, as they mostly are. The individual talents and specialist skills of highly trained team athletes are frustrated, diminished and wasted if there is no game plan which sets out to create the conditions where players have the opportunity to shine; and equally, vice-versa, focusing on the game plan will not produce success if the players are unfit. It is no different for an enterprise.

So which comes first – the pressing needs or the game plan – when both are needed and resources are limited? The answer lies in the fact that a new team in the league or one promoted from a lower grade seldom wins the premiership in the first year. Both have to be worked at. When a start is made on strengthening both, skills and game plans can be tested, evaluated, changed, honed and integrated over time into a polished, successful performance. Learning takes the path of a spiral.

Getting started

In spite of the day-to-day operational pressures in 1971, somehow we sensed that it was important to make a start on a game plan that would give us real long-term direction. This 'sense of the important' did not come from experience, because we had not previously travelled this path. But it is possible to identify three strands of influence which contributed to our decision to do it:

- My personal searching for direction had led me to thinking and reading about long-range planning for some years. I made a personal first attempt at this kind of activity by writing a long-range planning report and presenting it to the board in 1968. It would have been more accurately described as proposals for the next stage of company development with recommendations. But it did indicate a responsiveness to thinking about the future in a better way. Further, it did bear fruit over the following three years in response to two key recommendations, financial competence and training support. These, which have already been mentioned, then became the other two strands of influence.

- Our new finance director, with his fresh and penetrating approach broadened by experience in larger enterprises, understood the need and could see the potential for personal and company learning that would come from working on a game plan.

- Training support had come through David Lloyd-Thomas, a management consultant who, after some initial work with the company in 1970, was appointed consultant to the board. He was a marvellous teacher, contributing knowledge, insight and external objectivity from a breadth of consulting experience with medium to large corporations. He had been the catalyst for the team-building we had already undertaken by 1971 in the South Australian management group, that was to make a critical contribution to the company's survival in 1972. I had learnt so much from these development activities that I was enthusiastic to continue with this new assignment when David encouraged us to do so.

Conceiving a plan

So it happened that three colleagues and I embarked on the task which would produce the substance of the company's long-term direction. The instrument which we had been encouraged to adopt to provide structure to the task forced us to undertake some fast-track further education about fundamentals of organisation and business effectiveness. We needed to do so. I have observed that many people who start or manage small and medium sized businesses get into positions of leadership through being highly competent tradespersons, technicians or professionals. They have a strong grasp of those individual elements of the business which reflect their own discipline and work experience, but limited knowledge and understanding of others and how they all inter-relate to make up the whole enterprise. We were like that.

We were also to gain, along the way, more hands-on experience in the effort required to create conditions which will sustain effective participation. Many hours of reading and individual thinking about the company and how we believed it could perform best preceded the week we had set aside for intensive work together. The focus and particular objective or product of our labours was a set of written policy statements covering five key corporate elements of our business, elements which are common to most businesses, viz:

- scope and nature of the business
- financial objectives
- markets and marketing
- our people and their development
- organisation structure and function.

Taken together, they were described as an ideal corporate strategic model for operating and developing the company. These statements were to be cohesive and mutually supportive of each other and the whole, describing the kind of company we wanted to build. To keep our feet on the ground, we also examined with as much objectivity as we were able how we saw ourselves actually running the business when measured against these new standards. The following illustrations provide a pictorial representation of how we summarised our work and conclusions. The difference portrays opportunity for improvement. Contrast and comparison between the two models yielded the basic data from which we could determine priorities and make decisions and plans to move the company from its present state towards the goal we had designed.

By the time the task had been completed we had gained considerable knowledge and understanding, both theoretical and practical, about enterprises and how these could be applied to our own. We had also learnt a lot more from and about each other and how each thought

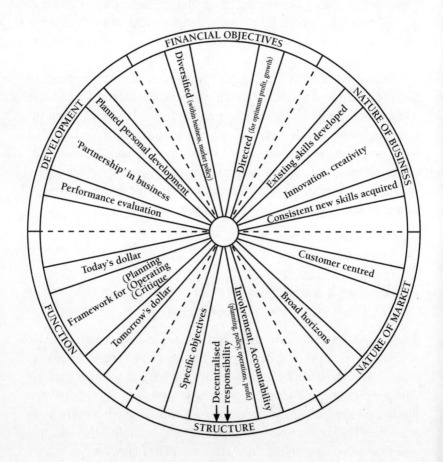

Baulderstone 1971: Aspirations – a model for the future.

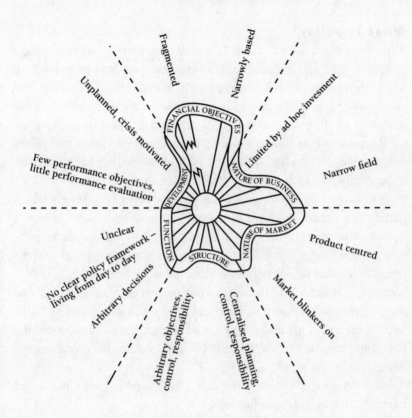

Baulderstone 1971: the model Bert and Bob had built!

about the parts and the whole of the business. Together we had produced a policy document which we believed was both sound and relevant to the company's future. In fact it proved to be of more lasting value than we could ever have expected. In 1989 a new leadership team repeated the task we had carried out in 1971 in order to deepen its common understanding of the policies which had guided the company to that point, and to evaluate their relevance to a much larger business and a different market place. Existing policy statements were subjected to rigorous critique with the choices of accepting, discarding, re-writing and adding new ones. Changes were made to clarify and strengthen the written words, but the substance was kept.

What is policy?

A question immediately arises. Is it really possible for an enterprise's policies to undergo so little change over a relatively long period during which the enterprise and market place have changed significantly, and still be valid and not signify a kind of corporate ossification? The possibility of an affirmative answer rests on what is meant by policy.

Three words commonly used in writing about how enterprises function are POLICY, PRACTICES and PROCEDURES. They are often used indiscriminately and carelessly. More often than not when the word 'policy' is used in conversation, the speaker is really talking about a particular practice, and sometimes even a procedure. It is, for example, not uncommon to hear comments like: 'Our policy is to purchase all cars from a single manufacturer.' This is a statement about current practice. It is not policy, because it does not help the decision-maker to continue to make sound decisions when market conditions change – as they frequently do for cars. Financial leases, operating leases, maintenance contracts, price wars and model changes have all influenced the decisions enterprises have made about their vehicle fleets over recent decades.

Baulderstone sought to bring clarity and discipline into its internal language through these definitions:

POLICY SUMMARY	describes the overall plan for achieving objectives in each selected corporate element of the business and identifies the key tactical approaches to achieve those objectives.
POLICY	sets the framework within which decisions are made and supports the overall plan.
PRACTICE	describes what is done. It represents a consistent way of applying policy in comparable situations.
PROCEDURE	describes how a task is done in detail.

PRACTICE and PROCEDURE	are tools for implementing policy. Standard practices and procedures are developed for those functions where standardisation increases overall efficiency.

Policy defined in this way and in this context is a vital contributor to creating conditions which will sustain effective participation. Effective participation means harnessing the often latent or under-used talents of our people by pushing decision-making down into the organisation. This is how delegation becomes an invitation to participate in leadership.

Policy and reality

An invitation to participate in leadership cannot be issued responsibly in a policy vacuum. Unacceptable levels of risk or organisational chaos are the most likely outcomes. It is more than a little ironic that, in 1971, we were about to learn this lesson the hard way. Just at the time we were completing our design for the company's future, the company's present started to crumble in Western Australia.

Was it a modern case of Nero fiddling? It would be easy to say so, perhaps too easy even if partially true. The time we had spent on this task did not worsen the pending crisis to any significant degree; its origins lay in other unsound decisions already described. What our endeavours did do was give to me and my finance director colleague a new depth of knowledge and understanding which supported us during those demanding days, enabling us to make the necessary decisions for survival while not completely losing sight of the better future we hoped might still be possible.

The company's ideal strategic model remained for five years within the close-knit circle of my immediate colleagues – until, as with the Baulderstone Philosophy, we had regained the confidence of our people and re-laid the groundwork for a new invitation to participate in leadership.

Making policy work

There is truth in the anonymous quip that 'the person who knows *what* to do will always have a job. The person who knows *why* will be the boss'.

It is the essence of sound policy that it disciplines the user/decision-maker to understand the reasons why a particular decision is made and why it is chosen against competing alternatives. When corporate policy is understood by decision-makers across the enterprise, a consistent application of policy becomes possible and authority can be widely disseminated in a way which promotes initiative but does not expose the enterprise to unacceptable risk. Understanding policy therefore becomes a prerequisite for this kind of involvement. I have become convinced that this is so, but also that policy development is a neglected and poorly understood element in business education.

1976 could be called our Year of the Game Plan. We took the step of involving the organisation in a new way in our thinking about the business, building on the firmer foundations we had more carefully laid. This year also marked the start of a decade of strong growth in construction competence, return on investment and company substance. In 1976:

- The Baulderstone Philosophy was issued and explained to all managers.
- The policy manual was reviewed and edited by the executive team in preparation for a series of education sessions with the whole middle management group in 1977.
- Information sessions, at six-monthly intervals, were commenced to which all staff employees, site leading hands and long-serving wages employees were invited.
- Teamwork-learning workshops were recommenced with a commitment to provide this opportunity to every existing and new staff employee.

Through the combination of these actions and activities, the company had begun to build its leadership development on strong, durable foundations. The leadership-and-the-bottom-step concept, which turns authoritarian approaches upside down, is illustrated below.

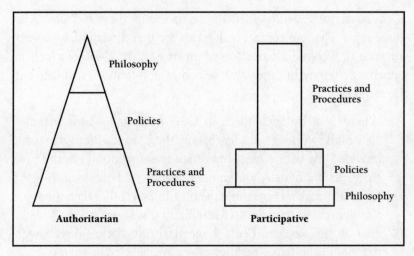

Philosophy and policy as the foundation of the business

The company had one philosophy in 1976, 47 policies and many more practices and procedures. The authoritarian diagram conveys a visual image of the one leader who knows what is best sitting at the pinnacle of knowledge and power. When leadership is encouraged throughout an organisation, philosophy provides the foundation and policy the structure on which decentralised operations can be confidently established.

Policy education in 1977 played an important part in the company's subsequent growth. It was a core contributor to frequent comments from customers and observers expressing surprise at the company's ability to provide an increasing number of competent project teams.

As a result of the experience of interactive sessions with middle managers, explanatory notes were included as part of the policy manual in order to strengthen ongoing understanding and application of policy. Policy education, however, is not a one-off exercise, a case of been there, done that. It requires constant reinforcement by executive managers at every opportunity, particularly by using policy as a standard for critique of every important decision made by themselves and their team members.

One of the middle managers who participated in these sessions was a young architect who joined the company in 1976 and stayed for three years. I had no contact with him since that time until, with great surprise, I received a letter from him in January 1998 in which he generously referred to the value he had gained from his involvement. He wrote:

> When I joined the company in 1976, I still had a fairly sheltered view of the world. I consider that my three years with the company provided me with a most important training ground both in the construction industry and in the general world of business.
>
> In particular, I remember the time in May 1977 when there was a minor recession in South Australia, and we were having our staff chat at the Redlegs Club. I recall sitting there, as you were describing the harsh realities of the prevailing commercial environment, thinking that at any moment you were about to invoke the 'last on – first off' rule or some similar medicine. Instead, you said that you felt that the company already had the best people in the industry, but that to survive we had to be better still. You then announced the commencement of the in-house training activities which were to be part of our Friday afternoons for the following years, and the value of which still remains.
>
> In that single move, you put the company ten years ahead of Bob Hawke's 'lucky country' speech, and in many instances, business in Australia is only just accepting training as a vital component.

Mutually supportive actions

The policy education program was just one way in which the executive group was building a partnership with middle managers. The circumstances of the early 1970s provided the opportunity to invite this group to become shareholders in the company and, progressively, to assist them financially to make it possible. Also, team-building experience was opening the way to much freer formal and informal communication about the company, its objectives, performance, achievements and problems.

Then we found that something more was needed. There is an old party game in which people stand in a large circle. One person whispers a message to a neighbour and this message is passed on from person to person round the circle until it returns to the initiator – by which time it is rarely the same message and frequently can barely be recognised. We had similar experiences at Baulderstone. Information that we wanted to share widely with staff and have them understand often arose out of the work of the executive group. Members of that group were responsible for conveying agreed information through their own teams to their parts of the organisation, a responsibility which would also assist in promoting openness and freeing up two-way communication. But this practice didn't always work as intended. As a result of listening to employees on field visits and during training sessions, I found that sometimes important items of information about the company had not got through, had been misunderstood, or produced different understanding in different parts of the business. This led to uncertainty and distraction that hindered performance.

Information sessions were our response to this concern. All staff would receive the same information in the same place twice a year. We aimed to provide a platform of common knowledge that would reduce the incidence of misunderstanding in ongoing workplace communication. Regular information sessions have been part of the company's practice ever since. Separate events are held in each geographical region as the company's activities have become dispersed but still with the same presenters at each location: the chief executive and the leaders of business units.

As sometimes happens, an action motivated by one need produces other benefits. Information sessions became a meeting place for employees across the company and its spread-out sites and operations, and for renewing past friendships and exchanging ideas. At the same time, they provided an informal setting for those employees with executive and director responsibilities to mingle, chat and listen.

A final observation. Encouraging managers, particularly the more senior managers, and requiring them to understand policy as the framework and discipline within which decisions are made forces them to learn about the business. It promotes personal growth and development. The impact on the whole business becomes an ever-present consideration in their specialist leadership roles. Policy used in this way significantly enhances the succession pool of potential candidates for positions of corporate leadership.

Chapter 13

DELEGATION

What does it mean?

While understanding policy affects the performance of all work teams, some directly and others indirectly, it is also true that a detailed knowledge of policy does not play a dominant part in the daily performance of them all. Delegation does.

Like 'policy', 'delegation' is a word used so widely and loosely that its meaning has been lost sight of and its practise weakened. How common it is to hear that someone is a workaholic because she or he can't delegate. Or manager Fred down the street just had a heart attack because he won't delegate. The thought behind such criticism is that the persons referred to won't offload any of their responsibilities. Another barrier to delegation is expressed in the saying: 'If you want a job done properly, do it yourself'. A consequence of adopting this approach is that the situation will never be any different because others are not given the encouragement, opportunity and guidance to learn.

To some, delegation means the boss telling subordinates what to do and checking that it has been done correctly. While this approach to involving others may be attractive because it is easier and can produce the best immediate results, two weaknesses stand out. It focuses the boss's effort on supervision of the work of others rather than personal contribution to results, and denies the subordinate opportunity to take initiative, develop and experience real satisfaction. If maintained, this approach also ensures that the situation will never be any different.

The dilemma is that this kind of delegating is often, if not mostly, easier in the short term. In contrast, delegation proper is the core means of achieving effective participation in every work team, and its principles apply equally to boardroom and shop floor. Delegation proper* takes effort, effort which is part of the task of building a genuinely participative organisation.

According to dictionaries, the word 'delegation' contains two ideas. If you are the manager doing the delegating, it means:

- the act of appointing another person to represent you, and
- committing functions or authority to that person to act as your agent.

One fact becomes immediately clear. The responsibility for the success of what is delegated remains clearly with the manager, even when it is shared with the representative or agent. Further, the dictionary does not define or explain delegation in terms of the boss–subordinate thinking referred to earlier. Representative and agent are inclusive terms. One person cannot represent another as agent if he or she does not understand precisely what the delegator wants to achieve and how the delegated assignment fits into the delegator's overall thinking.

Therefore, by definition, the word 'delegation' turns the boss–subordinate thinking on its head. Whatever action diagram (a) in the figure below represents, it isn't delegation. Diagram (b) portrays what the definition requires. This diagram is similar to that which appeared during the 1980s in business literature advocating 'service management'

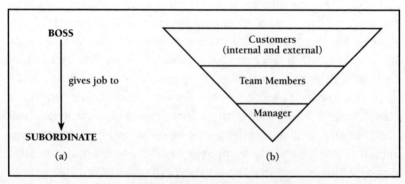

Delegation and service management are compatible

---

* The adjective 'proper' is not used in the rest of the text. 'Delegation' means delegation proper.

and customer-driven organisations. There is also a compatibility with
the participative model illustrated on page 85. The congruence that is
evident between these several ideas supports a conclusion that organisations which are genuinely participative will be best equipped to
deliver sustained high-standard customer service.

Making it work

Because the art of delegation was seen as such a vital link in moving
towards the design we had developed for the company, and because we
had learnt the hard way through earlier mistakes, we sought to cultivate
and reinforce through internal training the attitudes and practices
needed. We stressed the following principles:

1. Make sure each team member understands the objectives of
   your whole team so that he or she can fulfil the role of agent
   effectively.
   • Bring your whole team together for initial briefing.
   • Bring your whole team together at regular intervals for feedback on progress and critique of performance.

2. Define clearly the specific results that you expect each team
   member to achieve.
   • Set these objectives preferably by working together.
   • Agree standards for all aspects of the work.
   • Establish a plan to monitor progress.

3. Provide the support necessary to ensure that these results are
   achieved.
   • Use critique to strengthen solutions.
   • Keep in touch and provide informal feedback.
   • Conduct an end of activity critique.

When these conditions are not present, delegation becomes something else. Two possibilities are abdication and work-shedding.
Abdication contradicts the agent relationship in delegation and implies
that the manager acts as though he or she has no over-riding responsibility for the task or function given to the subordinate. The subordinate

is held responsible. In such situations it is literally true that the manager acts irresponsibly by failing to contribute through counsel, support, monitoring or critique. Work-shedding describes the situation where a manager, for any reason, off-loads work to subordinates because it is routine or of low personal interest or priority. The manager may still supervise what is done but little attempt is made to involve the subordinate in objectives, standards or critique. (Work-shedding should not, however, be confused with work-sharing, which is an action of team support where team members may take over part of a manager's work and the responsibility that goes with it, or vice-versa, in order to assist, for example, when the manager's work load is very great due to some short-term pressures.)

It is only too easy for a manager to slip into these bad practices, particularly when under pressure. Every manager should be vigilant.

Part of team action

The principles of delegation underline the importance of team action. The dimensions of responsibility discussed at the end of chapter eleven pervade its practise. The analogy of the sporting team again runs through the necessary conditions which have been identified – strategy briefings; roles and contribution based on the particular strengths and expertise of individual players; most of the play occurring by team members individually, in pairs or small groups; and debriefing after the match to improve the next game.

The role of manager can be compared to a combination of captain and coach. The manager firstly needs to lead by example, a player in the team using his or her particular skills and experience to contribute to the end result. The manager's other role is that of coach: consultant, educator, extender of horizons, encourager, supporter, colleague, and sometimes confronter.

In all the ways described delegation conveys to every employee the message that they are valued. Delegation also conveys the invitation and opportunity to take initiative and accept responsibility and so participate in the leadership of the enterprise.

The focus of this chapter has been on giving authority to team members for decisions, tasks and results which can be delegated, and on what makes delegation effective. One important principle remains to be emphasised. Every leader/manager in the role of team player must also decide **what will not be delegated**. There are always a small number of issues which are critical in their potential to impact for good or ill on the achievement of the team's overall objectives in terms of results and standards. Decisions affecting these few issues should not be delegated.

Part 4

MUTUALITY

Openness to Each Other

We strive to create conditions in which every employee is challenged and encouraged to excel, where personal goals can be matched with the goals of the business, and where we all accept responsibility for the property and reputation of the Group.

Chapter 14

INTERLUDE

This chapter reproduces the text of an address I gave to the South Australian Division of the Institution of Engineers Australia on 17 March 1992 at the launching of an industry support scheme for unemployed graduates.

One of the things for which I am most grateful in my working life is that for ten years I had a mentor. For ten years, as the company for which I was responsible struggled to retain its place and grow from a medium-sized builder in the small economic pool of this State into a national constructor, a short, dapper Welshman with a large moustache and razor-sharp mind who was ten years my senior was progressively consultant, adviser, educator, colleague, confronter, supporter and, as a result of these shared experiences, close personal friend.

In the early 1970s some contracts in the Pilbara in Western Australia went wrong and brought the company to the verge of bankruptcy, providing one of my most difficult work and life experiences. In the midst of that experience, my mentor said to me, 'I know people who would give their right arm to be gaining your experience'. I hardly agreed at the time!

In his own expressive way, my mentor was rephrasing two cryptic and often repeated quotations that contain a good measure of wisdom:

- Experience is what you get when you don't get what you wanted
- Success is the ability to survive failure.

I would not presume to suggest to those of you who are having difficulty finding employment that this experience of mine is similar to yours. Comparisons in this kind of situation are not appropriate. But I would encourage you to reflect on the wisdom contained in those two cryptic sentences because they are expressions of hope.

Mentors and *hope*. These are words that are inherent in the initiative that has motivated this gathering.

'Hope' is a strong word for one of the most important characteristics of all human endeavour. It is regrettable that it has been much discounted by everyday use to nearer the level of wishful thinking, a kind of lottery for living. Hope is what sustains in us the vision that improvement is possible. Through hope, we continue to strive for better ways of living, working and relating. Through hope, we maintain confidence in our capacity to change, to grow and to influence those better ways, provided that we *choose* to strive, grow and influence ... and provided, also, that we have some support and encouragement in our endeavours – for no man nor woman is an island. Hope therefore calls forth both self-reliance *and* support.

One message I would like to see our educators and communicators write indelibly on the minds of every emerging generation is the historical truth that **no generation has ever been able to influence the conditions into which is has been born**. So, those born in the late 1960s or the 1970s have not been able to influence the fact that they face a degree of employment uncertainty not seen in Australia for sixty years. Similarly, people born in the last years of the nineteenth century and twenty years later were not able to influence the fact that they were born to a degree of war and death not since repeated. And if we should look at countries other than Australia in our turbulent world, the axiom would be the same, only probably more dramatically presented.

Whenever we create an expectation that future generations will not or should not have to face hardship in some form, we also say to them that we do not believe that they have the will, the skill and the courage to do so. We do them, and in Australia we have been doing them, a great disservice.

Six years ago I had the opportunity to talk briefly with Australian author Morris West when he visited Adelaide to deliver a public lecture. He had just published *Cassidy*, a story written around corruption in high places in this country ... a somewhat prophetic theme looking back over these last six years of royal commissions into corruption. He said to me that sometimes it is easier for people to recognise unpalatable facts (where recognition is the first stage of facing up) when those facts are parcelled in a fiction or art form, than if they are just baldly stated.

When some years later I saw a video of the film *Lean on me*, based on the true story of the influence of a headmaster of a run-down, out-of-control high school for black students in New Jersey, I was reminded of what Morris West had said. I felt that the film had the potential to say something we need to hear.

The headmaster places responsibility unequivocally on each student with the words: 'If you don't succeed in life, I want you to blame yourselves; not your parents, not history, not your hard luck, not the white man ...' But he does not leave it there. He backs what he says with his life, which consistently conveys the message, 'Lean on Me'.

The industry support scheme being launched this evening calls for self-reliance from the graduate and support from the employed and the employers. It is a scheme to reinforce hope and to foster the mentor relationship. Those who have conceived it have laid simple, practical and realistic foundations on which participants can build. There is direction through guidelines but room for adaptation and creativity to get the best value from each individual relationship. It is *mutual* in terms of responsibility and in the potential for both parties to receive benefits. It takes two to tango.

So to those of you who may become graduate participants I would like to say two things, with sensitivity to your particular circumstances but a directness born out of personal experience. Firstly, if you don't succeed in life, which includes making participation in this scheme worthwhile for you, don't blame the organisation, nor the economy, nor your rotten luck, nor anything nor anyone . . .

Secondly, think about those words: 'Experience is what you get when you don't get what you wanted.' What are you learning from this time in your life? If you have time on your hands now, maybe it will be the only period in your life over the next 30 years or more when this will be so. It is not a wasted period in your life – nor a period to be wasted.

And to you who are employed engineers or employers, I would like to say these three things. Firstly, there is no way you can justifiably excuse your organisation for not being a participant in this scheme. It is simple, practical and low in financial cost. Secondly, every action taken in Australia that strengthens self-reliance and gives encouragement and support, as does this scheme, adds something to national productivity; and sometimes it could happen that your support will enable some future genius of invention or innovation to regain confidence and motivation – then that something becomes substantial. Thirdly, at the human and personal level there is a very Australian characteristic in the mentor relationship – a particular kind of mateship. There are few achievements that give more lasting satisfaction than knowing that a younger brother or sister sustained or regained his or her confidence and self-reliance because, when it was needed, you were able to say, 'Lean on Me.'

Chapter 15

STRUCTURE FOR LEARNING

Breaking the shackles

Everyone needs some luck in life and in business. My first meeting with David Wynn Lloyd Lloyd-Thomas, who could hardly have been anything but Welsh, came by a rather serendipitous pathway, a chance encounter.

The Baulderstone board had before it at the beginning of 1969 a recommendation 'that competitive offers be obtained from several recognised management consultants' to help us establish a sound in-company training program that would be on-going. This recommendation was not founded on the belief that management consultants could or should run our training on a continuous basis, but on our stop-start performance through the 1960s which provided compelling evidence that we needed some help to get started. So the board finally agreed.

The brief and letters of invitation to five consultant firms whom I believed would have the experience and Adelaide-based resources to help us had been prepared and despatched. It was just then that I received a letter from David's company, unknown interstate consultants, announcing the opening of an office in Adelaide. Their letter stated that they specialised in management development and training. I recall thinking, 'What the hell!' and sent out another invitation. I later learnt that this new office was only a shopfront prompted by the transfer to Adelaide of the spouse of one of their staff members.

I was searching for a way forward and seeking assistance from outside the company. However, I did understand a core part of our problem. We had already sent four middle managers to ten-day live-in executive staff courses, a considerable investment for a business of our size. I had seen them return animated and enthusiastic, only to watch with disappointment and frustration this new vitality gradually being snuffed out by the day-to-day job demands and the reluctance of their co-workers to support and encourage them to apply their learning. Each was a severe case of 'fade-out'.

Experience had been teaching us a fundamental principle of organisation building. **If an enterprise wants to improve its performance through improving the skills and productivity of its people, it must at the same time make the environment within the enterprise responsive to change, to new ideas, and different and better ways of doing things.** Or, to use the management profession's language, strategic thinking and a supportive culture go hand in hand. In applying technical innovation and introducing better construction methods and equipment we had made significant steps forward, but our progress was painfully slow in developing leadership and increasing capacity for control and independence amongst our people. Yet I couldn't see how to do it better.

In this, I was not alone. I soon discovered that fewer than half the consultants we approached understood our dilemma or tried seriously to address it. So my first meeting with David remains etched on my memory. He was short, not Australian, sported a handle-bar moustache and had a hyphenated name! An unlikely companion whose first impression needled my prejudices. But then he listened, intently. And when he spoke he focused immediately on my needs and concerns; he conveyed clearly that he understood my vision and desires for the company. To find someone who understands in that way is a special gift. My frustration and the barriers to improving performance were straight away halved and the possibilities doubled because they were genuinely shared. In those days it still seemed a big risk to engage a firm where the consultants all lived 700 kilometres away. But the choice had already been made. David had no competitors when it came to understanding.

Taking the plunge

Following that first meeting, David sent me a copy of *Corporate Darwinism*, by Dr Robert Blake, Dr Jane Mouton and Warren Avis, the founder of the Avis Corporation. This short work dramatically mirrored the experience of Baulderstone as it had moved from the founder phase into the managed business phase (while still retaining characteristics of the family company) and was searching for something better. This something better *Corporate Darwinism* called 'the dynamic corporation'. I was 37, stimulated and excited by this possible way forward.

Training as an integral part of the company's operations began in May 1970 with a two-day conference organised and guided by our appointed consultants. Forty of the company's staff – almost all of its managers, supervisors and foremen – worked in groups to examine the impact of communication and management controls on productivity with the objective of identifying development and training needs. It was a start and led on to further training in specific subject areas. Looking back now, I think it was a good start, certainly a better start than I understood then. It introduced our middle management to completely new ways of participation, formulating plans that would involve them all. It was a big step forward in thinking, but also a small step in building their confidence and commitment.

When I reviewed the outcomes of this event and experience with David, he said that he believed the best course for Baulderstone was to get involved in a Grid program. He spoke of the Managerial Grid, the learning instrument designed by Blake and Mouton and tested for practical usefulness during the late 1950s and early 1960s. It was their response to the problem posed to them by enterprises which were seeking to become more productive and dynamic. David had a vested interest in his proposed best course – his consultancy business held the licence for the Grid in Australia. However, I was an enthusiastic starter following my reading of *Corporate Darwinism* and was able to encourage and persuade the seven managers who reported to me – some were less than enthusiastic – to attend a Grid seminar. We launched into the deep.

I still consider the five days spent at that seminar in 1970 to have been my most valuable learning experience, because it opened my mind and my eyes in two important ways. Each became a doorway to expanding opportunities and possibilities for the company and me personally. I began to get a picture of teamwork and how teams work. Learning from the good and bad performances of my seminar team, I also began to understand what ingredients could produce high-quality team results and what attitudes, behaviour and methods of approach created significant barriers.

The second way in which my eyes were opened was more personal and underlined one principle presented at the seminar which I have found true to all working relationships. **Actions which can be observed, not good intentions, determine the results of people working together.**

Being reserved and reflective by nature, I had acquired the frequent habit of listening to but not making any response to the contribution of others. I would be thinking about it, evaluating it, but not giving any clue to what I thought or concluded. While I had the very best of intentions in my desire to be a strong team contributor, my lack of response was mostly interpreted as non-acceptance or dismissal. This had been a barrier in the work of the seminar team where we were all equals and from different enterprises. How much more of a barrier to willing contribution was it likely to have been in my own team, where I was also seen as 'the boss'?

While this incident might be viewed as a relatively small piece of learning, even insignificant, its impact was far reaching. By opening my eyes to the consequences of my unresponsiveness, I started to learn to listen and how to promote more constructive two-way communication. My life and understanding were enriched, colleagues were encouraged and team performance gained from the increased contribution from its members. These kinds of benefits continue to multiply.

My team made this observation near the end of the seminar during an activity in which team members worked together to help each see in what ways he or she could grow to become a more effective leader/manager. Every person can be helped in their personal development and effectiveness by feedback of this kind. The feedback was based solely on the experience gained within the team during the intensive activities of the seminar, but was remarkably accurate and relevant to my work team. It was possible because of the levels of trust and openness which had by then developed, and the safeguards in the process. It was an experience of rich mutuality, a special privilege as well as a serious responsibility.

Choosing a tool of trade

Because of the personal experience just described and the choice the company was to make following it, this story requires some further brief comments about the Managerial Grid.

The Grid is an instrument of learning designed to help an enterprise focus on the dimension of mutuality, on how the enterprise might involve its people in the business in order to produce better long-term results. When the Grid was first introduced into the market place in 1964 in the United States (several years later in Australia), it presented a new development in management education; the importance of this dimension of mutuality was rarely heard of then. This contrasts with the huge groundswell of social and professional support for such a concept over the last two decades, which have yielded a plethora of authors, texts and competing instruments and approaches proffering solutions for building culture, teamwork and participation. However, making it happen doesn't seem to have become any easier and the rhetoric frequently seems to have been lost in a relentless pursuit of such fashionable ends as 'downsizing' and 'outsourcing'.

Baulderstone chose the Grid because it was available and offered, and its application addressed the core difficulty encountered in the company's earlier experience. I quickly came to see it as a tool to help us build a better business, to make tangible strides 'towards excellence'. It is not a tool which yields perfect results any more than a carpenter's plane is a perfect instrument or ensures a smooth finish irrespective of the skill of the user. We had to learn how to use it and we made mistakes, but gradually we gained understanding of its strengths and limitations. Not every participant obtained real value or became an advocate, but my judgement of our experience is that it served the company well. Baulderstone stayed with the Grid over three decades for seven reasons. These seven reasons provide a checklist for choosing any learning approach.

1. **It had the support and direct interest of the chief executive.**

2. **Company performance improved.**
   Improvements were noticeable in terms of project results, growth and return on investment. Strong morale and a steady growth in the number of highly competent project teams could be linked with Grid-based team-building.

3. **It provided a learning experience across the company.**
   A common experience of this kind provides a platform which encourages team members and teams to continue learning. It facilitates the formation of new teams. From 1976 every supervisor, technician and manager who joined the company was offered the opportunity to attend an in-company Grid seminar. A supportive enterprise culture requires some critical mass.

4. **The knowledge gained was practical and relevant.**
   In the in-company seminars we worked hard to achieve real understanding of the principles, behaviour and skills which underpin Grid learning – such as goals, convictions, planning, usage of time, communication, preparation, problem-solving, conflict, self-awareness, critique. The learning-by-doing context strengthens integration and relevance.

5. **It proved versatile and adaptable.**
   Grid instruments were applied to improving the performance of existing work teams such as business unit leadership teams. Principles were adapted to workshops developed by the company to strengthen cohesion in newly established company project teams for large contracts, and to build greater cohesion and purpose in multi-disciplinary teams which included

representatives of the company, the customer and other participating organisations (such as architects and consulting engineers). They were also adapted, when the environment permitted, to the process of facilitating enterprise agreements with the unionised workforce.

6. **It was not superficial.**
The Grid's values and principles proved sound and the experience gained had congruence with 'real life'; it made sense. Most of the learning was just as valid and useful outside the business as at work. It is multi-cultural in the sense that Grid seminars have been conducted in almost every continent in the world with beneficial results. Its founders, Drs Blake and Mouton, had credibility and were recognised for their work through their election to the American Management Hall of Fame in December 1987.

7. **It was safe for participants.**
Our experience with many in-house seminars confirmed this. The Grid's focus is on changing the way people work together by changing individual and group understanding, behaviour and attitudes, not personality.

Challenged to excel

I first read the words 'corporate excellence' in *Corporate Darwinism* and knew immediately that they encapsulated the objective for which I had been searching, but had been unable to articulate. They gave expression to my personal ambitions and my unclear aspirations for Baulderstone, and in so doing sharpened their focus and bite.

Having or creating the motivation to do better is at the heart of continuous improvement. The simple diagram below illustrates this characteristic of changes which we desire and intend to bring about. It represents an approach which is adopted in all the Grid instruments of organisation and team-building. It also has general application to virtually every situation of human achievement.

Baulderstone's record of technical development through the 1960s shows that the company was not without either goals or pathway. However, the record also shows that the starting place was not as favourable as we liked to think, the goal further away than a naïve optimism perceived and the pathway more strewn with hazards than we were willing or able to identify and anticipate. The Grid instruments were designed to challenge easy first perceptions and solutions and made us think through and face up to more of the disciplines, opportunities and difficulties in each component of this undertaking – that is, what it would take to build an excellent enterprise. They made us test whether we were really serious and up to a challenge to excel. As a result, we were much better equipped to make sustainable progress in the 1970s than the 1960s, and we did.

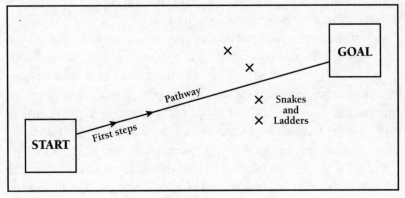

A simple, universal model for improvement

Through the struggles implicit in these endeavours, we began to understand some of the basic essentials inherent in all aspirations for personal and organisational development. The simple disciplines encouraged us to tackle that development with something more promising than haphazard trial and error.

Almost every personal development goal requires changes in behaviour for its fulfilment – such as changes in attitudes, what is done, how it is done. These introduce a dimension of uncertainty, for we will be traversing new ground. We may, therefore, have difficulty describing 'the goal' in terms which are helpful to making progress even though we have a notion, a dream, a feeling about what we really want to achieve. The challenge is to imagine, to speculate, to make an hypothesis about what our dream might actually look like if we can forget for the moment the constraints of the present. This then becomes our best possible picture of our goal – a picture which can be sharpened or reshaped as we gain experience and make progress. It is the soundest description we can make at the time of our ideal for the future.

It is one thing to take on this task as an individual person; it becomes considerably more complex and demanding for a group or an enterprise and it is easy to get trapped in a talk-fest. We found that Grid instruments made us work more and talk less. They provided a framework for thinking about the future which helped us to consider alternative possibilities in direction and action and the likely consequences of each on people, performance and results.

Describing the present situation or condition – ie where we are now – is a more daunting challenge. If it is a case of our own development, we will be tempted to see our starting point as made up of our good intentions and other subjective perceptions. As an example, what my seminar team had told me about not responding to the contributions of other team members was, in my life outside the business, a difficulty which had been hampering communication in our marriage for years. Even though Judy and I had talked about it, on numerous occasions, I confess, I couldn't and wouldn't hear (both contributed) until I heard the message clearly from elsewhere. Joseph Conrad, in his masterly tale *Lord Jim*, sums up this human complaint: 'For it is my belief no man ever understands quite his own artful dodges to escape from the grim shadow of self-knowledge'.

When the situation involves not just one person but a group who work together or a whole organisation, the dilemma is compounded and the task of defining where we are now presents a great challenge. To get an accurate fix on the enterprise's present location requires all those skills which make teams work. We were greatly assisted by having a framework and method of approach which kept us focused in spite of many divergent points of view and distractions.

We discovered that when people do participate in the searching analysis that produces valid and useful descriptions of a soundest destination and a realistic actual-now status, they gain real knowledge and understanding about what currently is and what could be possible. In these circumstances, the contrast generates real motivation to change. Lasting change for the better is not possible without such motivation. The history of athletic achievement provides many examples confirming this. The story of how the four-minute mile was eventually broken is a classic one.

Motivation expresses itself in progress. The longest journey begins with a single step. There are no giant leaps to utopia. People who set unrealistic goals for progress in personal or organisational development may rightly be seen as creating their own conditions for failure, which can then become the justification for not trying. It is only a little further along that not trying becomes cynicism, perchance despair. Though the goal stretches far ahead, the first steps are vital – specific practical actions which I or we can take now, and thereby recognise movement. Progress reinforces motivation.

Finally, it is necessary to anticipate the barriers and the straight ways which are always part of the landscape, the 'snakes and ladders' that can hinder or speed progress towards the goal.

Chapter 16

OPERATING SYSTEM

A computer analogy

The performance of an enterprise is not determined solely by its team-work and team skills. They may not even be the predominant factors. The role of teamwork and team skills is to keep on enhancing performance, getting the very best from the people and resources available.

My simplified layman's understanding of how a computer works is illustrated below. The built-in operating system of the computer hardware provides the means, speed and flexibility by which competent users of high-quality application software make best use of the data available.

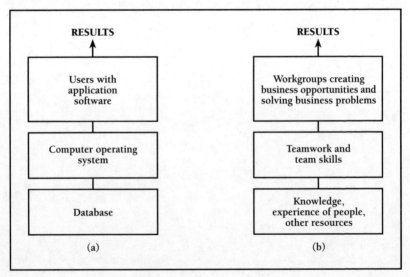

A computer analogy – teamwork as operating system

Quality software and a high-class operating system will not produce high-quality results if the database is flawed. On the other hand, a flawless database will yield mediocre results if the operating system is too slow or limited to take advantage of this potential.

In a similar way, how the strategic planning and operating components of an enterprise make use of the knowledge, experience and skills of their people is dependent on the quality of the teamwork and team skills which have been built into the enterprise. It remains true that high-quality teamwork cannot deliver outstanding performance if the enterprise's people do not have the competence, innovation and creativity needed to compete. Conversely, the talents of outstanding people and good people can lie dormant or wasted if the enterprise does not deliberately foster and make use of them.

Teamwork and team skills provide a key to open wide the talent bank. Though teamwork has many facets and there are a multitude of team skills, I have come to see four attitude/skill combinations as foundational: the openness to hear, to see, to discover, to learn. Without these it is rarely possible to get to the heart of any issue in an enterprise of size, whether it is an opportunity or problem, strategic or operational matter. These four elements provide progressive building blocks for each other and become collectively reinforcing. Much has been written on these subjects, but this story would be incomplete without a brief summary of characteristics drawn from hard-learned experience.

Open to hear

In his book *Love, Power and Justice*, Paul Tillich presents the axiom: 'No human relation ... is possible without mutual listening.' An enterprise which aspires to excel has no alternative but to make itself a listening organisation: listening to customers and partners from outside; mutual listening along and across levels of responsibility within. It is the first skill of team-building. To give to another the courtesy of genuinely listening is the simplest and most basic mark of respect. Therefore it supports or undermines every play – the individual alone, pairs, trios, task groups and the whole. It either blocks or frees up contributions, new ideas, opportunities and awareness of problems.

As with other talents or aptitudes, some people are by nature better listeners than others. But as again for every natural ability, the best listeners are those who have continued to develop that capacity. Most of us are not good listeners by nature. But we can all become effective listeners by cultivating helpful attitudes and habits and overcoming undisciplined behaviour which creates barriers. We can choose to listen.

The way we listen discloses our purpose. Are we listening to pick an argument, score a point, find a weakness, gain an advantage or because we can't avoid it? Or do we want to hear and understand so that we can be a friend, provide the right service to a customer, solve a problem, discover a new idea? It is important to know the difference.

As one not gifted with the innate talent of a keen listener, I found three suggestions helpful to making practical progress: listen actively, give feedback and learn how to ask questions.

Active listening is involvement with the speaker in his or her conversation. It encourages others to continue speaking while enabling you, the listener, to be confident that you understand what is being said. Insight can be strengthened by contrasting active listening with other kinds of listening: for example, passive listening, as occurs when our concentration is half-hearted – we are reading the paper, say, and thinking about the news and make little effort to engage or encourage the speaker; defensive listening, when our mind is on the response we wish to make – 'Yes, but ...' is a common give-away; aggressive listening, where the objective is to knock down what is being said, diminish both message and speaker; filtered listening, where our prejudices, values, attitudes and past experiences come to the fore and permit only selected parts of the message to get through.

Giving feedback enables the listener to avoid, or at least significantly reduce, the traps and temptations to fall into passive, defensive, aggressive or filtered listening. Telling the speaker what you have understood shows that you are listening and provides the opportunity to have your understanding confirmed or clarified. Other kinds of feedback encourage more detailed explanations, such as the phrases 'I'm interested, tell me more', or 'Do you mean ...?'

Constructive questions provide focus and promote understanding. Your competence as a communicator can be greatly enhanced by studying and practising such different approaches as closed-ended questions, which may illicit facts in response to Are ...?, Who ...?, When ...?, Where ...?, but tend to close off conversation; open-ended questions, which prompt explanation and interest and, in contrast, may start with How ...?, Why ...?, In what way ...?; clarifying questions; synthesising questions, which aim to add new information and build on what others have said; validating questions, which frequently make use of the important discipline of contrast and comparison.

Within an enterprise, listening is the most important skill in bringing about mutual recognition of goals and responsibility. When it is possible to match personal goals with company goals, motivation and commitment to desired results are self-generating, while the momentum from being in it together yields the added dividend of a shared responsibility for property and reputation.

This is a result worth striving for even if it is an ideal. It will not be possible to match the real personal goals or ambitions of every employee with those of the business. It may be possible to go most of the way for a few. However, every employee can be encouraged to think about how their job might contribute to their own development and their future aspirations, whether these lie within or outside the work place. When an enterprise through its leadership at all levels genuinely talks with and listens to its employees about careers and personal development, it is surprising what new practical possibilities emerge within existing circumstances. I know this from experience. An inherent consequence of the enterprise's demonstrated concern for the development of its people is increased motivation, commitment and responsibility for the work in hand.

Likewise, the ability to listen to each other becomes the foundation for designing simple, workable systems (which people will use, not just go through the motions) for maintaining on-going objectives and regular review of performance.

Open to see

Openness to see is an extension of openness to hear.

When people who work together start to listen to each other with a greater intention to understand, it is possible, even likely, that more disagreement, not less, will be the result. For example, with a show of interest, a reticent member of the group may be encouraged to contribute where there was little or no contribution before. And his or her views might be at odds with those of others or ones established already in the group. Or each group member, with probing questions and feedback, may begin to contribute more frankly, to say what he or she really feels or thinks, not just what they might have seen as acceptable and comfortable.

Will the outcome be confusion and frustration? Or will it be progress? Teamwork requires that team members learn how to deal constructively with conflict. A good starting point is to accept that conflict is inevitable, the product of our diversity. Accepting this fact will help to moderate feelings such as guilt and irritation. If conflict is inevitable, it is probable that it is not all bad, and just possible that it can be good. It is not the existence of conflict but how it is handled which determines whether its effect will be destructive or constructive.

Conflict always provides an opportunity for testing and strengthening authenticity and understanding. The skills of the team and its members will determine whether these opportunities are grasped or lost; whether the issue is settled with one side winning and another losing with attendant resentment, or through a less-than-happy compromise; or whether the team has gained a better outcome and everyone has learned through the experience.

If three conditions are present, work teams and their enterprises will be equipped to get the best results when conflict inevitably arises. These are that:

- the quality of solutions takes precedence over status
- listening skills are sufficient to work through differences
- team support is used to overcome impasses.

When the team is committed to getting the best solution, differences are confronted on the grounds of *what* is right or best, not *who* is right. When differences are resolved on the basis of status, whether it is the status of rank, service, qualifications, bullying power or whatever, understanding and commitment are diminished and the solution compromised. The conflict has ceased but not disappeared even when the resulting decision or course of action turns out to have been the best possible at the time.

While learning to listen is likely to bring to the surface more disagreement, learning to listen better is the way towards clearer vision. Conflict was no stranger in any of my own work teams. Occasions arose where conflicting views about an issue important to the team caused tension and wasted time, only for us to find out eventually that the conflict was more a result of misunderstanding than real. Individual team members must take listening seriously, so they become open to seeing issues from each other's point of view. Literally, listening means to list, to lean towards the speaker mentally and emotionally in order to understand the speaker's meaning and where the speaker is coming from. Such listening involves the perspective of empathy, of moving for the moment away from our own position and point of view to stand where the other stands. The figure below makes the point in an extreme illustration where A swears the ball is black and B swears that it is white. Both seem right from where they stand, while the simple way to resolve the conflict is for each to move towards the other's place.

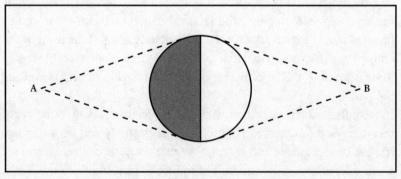

Illustrating perspective

I recall one incident which illustrates the relevance of perspective. A bricklaying subcontractor's performance became a serious problem at a time when there was an industry shortage of bricklayers, threatening a project's timely completion. It was a difficult problem to fix without increasing the cost, and I discussed it with the project manager, who was normally reliable. When the problem continued to become more critical, I confronted him again, stressing his accountability. A few days later he asked to see me and offered to resign. I was perplexed by his attitude, and certainly his resignation would hardly help the project or the company at that point. However, it was the catalyst for discovering the position from which he was coming. He was Polish and had joined the company immediately upon arrival in Australia in the 1970s from his home land. His inability to recruit more bricklayers at reasonable cost and my stressing his accountability had raised spectres from his former work experiences in communist Poland. He had become paralysed and uncommunicative through fear of reprisal. When I understood this, it was possible to deal with his fear and he soon fixed the problem to our mutual satisfaction.

Remaining aware of the influence of perspective in communication helps us discern whether conflict is primarily conflict caused by feelings arising from past or present experience, conflict of position or function, or the conflict of competing ideas and alternative directions. The conflict of competing ideas arising from strong personal convictions grounded on knowledge and experience contains the sparks of creativity, the synergy that can lead to a best solution. Conflict of position or function (eg sales versus production, business development versus finance) must be tested against the over-arching goals of the team or the enterprise; this is a particular instance where team members gain understanding and accept responsibility for the whole as well as the part.

Conflict which is primarily based on feelings about other team members or the subject is a barrier to both creativity and performance. It must be recognised and accepted so that it can be dealt with and set aside in order to make progress. Conflict arising from prejudice is a severe form which must be confronted. Near the end of the timeless film *Twelve Angry Men*, Henry Fonda, who has the lead role, explains why: 'Whenever we come across it, prejudice always obscures the truth.'

Conflict in work teams at any particular time, whether team members are together in one place or not, mostly occurs between two members or some members of the team. The temptation is for other members to sit on the side lines, ignore it or turn off. This is an irresponsible act. Every team member shares responsibility for the effectiveness of the team. Allowing those involved time to work through the issue causing conflict themselves is sometimes the best course, but long hold-ups or continuing barriers caused by conflict between some team members hampers team effectiveness. Team support in the form of constructive contribution or intervention, often by an observant and perceptive team member who has greater insight into what is actually happening, is an essential part of achieving excellent results.

Being open to see is the only path to 'facing-up'. Facing-up means seeing things as they are, not better, not worse. Facing-up as a core attitude and expectation within the culture of the team or enterprise is one of the most difficult qualities first to achieve and then to maintain. Yet it is absolutely critical in determining whether the most important problems get addressed. The age of problems in any enterprise is therefore a good indicator of the practice of facing-up. The demand for increased performance and productivity in government-owned authorities and departments over the last decade or so, and the consequent large reductions in the number of employees, has frequently been credited to or blamed mostly on the so-called political philosophy of 'economic rationalism'. Irrespective of how well or poorly these changes have been handled, little recognition has been given to a root of the problem – the support given to overstaffing by successive past leadership over decades.

Facing-up is the opposite to saving face, and this points to another axiom of great importance. **It is not possible to create a culture of openness where there is also a culture of blame.** If openness is to be seen as a strength without which teamwork is not possible, then the nature and quality of shared responsibility which it engenders must deliver a level of accountability that greatly exceeds the 'sheeting it home' demands of the autocratic leader, or the 'finding a scapegoat' ones of the politically driven enterprise. The trail for achieving this passes through the ways in which appointment, induction, agreeing objectives and standards, and reviewing performance and delegation are practised. Ironically, where a culture of blame exists or develops, it is likely that there has been little facing-up or sheeting home of responsibility for establishing quality in these practices which provide the necessary support for a just and genuine accountability.

Open to discover

Commitment, not agreement, is the essence of consensus.

Any enterprise which aspires to excel will never be short of problems requiring solutions. Continuous improvement means the continuing search for better solutions in every part of the business. It is a never-ending engagement with discovery. Progress relies on creative problem-solving, the word 'problem' being used generically to denote any issue, opportunity or circumstance that requires a decision, ie a solution. The emphasis I give to 'creative' stresses the willingness to search for a new solution which might be better than one proposed by any individual. This kind of problem-solving, where more than one person has a stake in the outcome and a role in achieving it, relies on the openness to hear and the openness to see of the team members involved. This is important not only in the formulation of the best solution, but because the best solution only remains the best if the quality of the implementation matches the quality of the decision. Implementation relies on commitment, often the commitment of a whole team.

Most problems which can have a significant impact on an enterprise have a number of dimensions and involve a number of streams or disciplines. Consider, for example, the strikes on the Australian waterfront in response to moves towards privatisation which dramatically disrupted trade and export in Australia over many months in the late 1990s and caused a serious problem for the stevedores, commerce, trade, government, waterside-workers, individual farmers and businesses. How should this problem be defined? Was it fundamentally a problem about attitudes, or the system, or about power and control, or different objectives and interests? And what was its cause? Was it simply the greed of one party or another? Was the whole industrial relations system unworkable? Did some want to preserve the system because of their influence over it and some want to destroy it for a different kind of self interest? Was it . . .?

Whether these would have been the right questions for the particular example is not here important. What is important is that questions of this kind need to be posed and answered. The answers given or the answers assumed (ie what happens when the questions are not posed) will radically affect the solution that is developed. Therefore the chain of creative problem-solving illustrated below starts with the principle: **make sure the problem which is to be solved is understood**. While this may seem ludicrously elementary, in practice it is not; western culture has established a vision of leadership much more strongly disposed to action of the get-into-it-and-fix-it-quick kind than one directed firstly to analysis and understanding. Experience shows that when it is assumed as self-evident or taken for granted that the problem or task is understood, particularly if it is complex, many mistakes, errors of judgement and half-baked or misdirected solutions and plans result. The wasted millions in developing computer technology in many enterprises of all kinds is a telling illustration.

It is possible to test this proposition with a simpler and more common example. Think for a moment about a confrontation between a parent and child who does not want to go to school. Imagine you are the parent. How easy it is to jump to conclusions about the reasons why. You may be influenced by your own feelings at the time, what other pressures you are under (eg time, other children, personal distress), your prejudices or the fact that this has happened before. Very similar influences can cause us to make faulty assumptions about more complex problems and go tearing up the wrong creek.

Conversely, if we address ourselves with rigour and as a priority to the first step of defining the problem in detail, the whole process, as well as the result, benefits. A significant problem needs to be understood in terms of its nature (is it about attitudes, methods, technology, financial impact, increasing profit, decreasing cost?); its extent (how far

GETTING IT RIGHT FIRST TIME ALL THE TIME

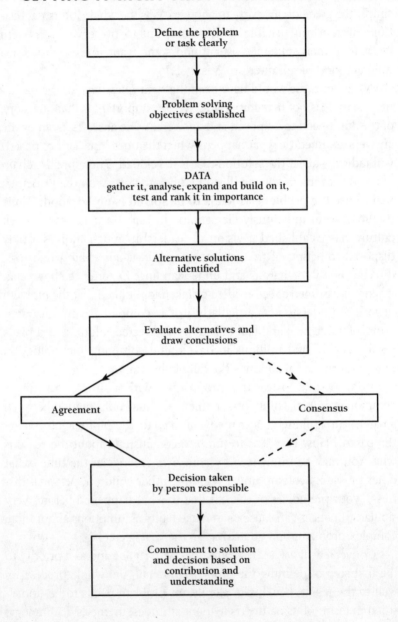

Creative problem-solving

do its tentacles extend – across the team, project, department, enterprise, beyond?); its impact (in terms of dollars, morale, delays, reputation); its probable causes; and what problem-solving objectives might be set. Even making decisions about relatively simple problems can benefit from a few minutes of this kind of discipline.

When a team searches for such an understanding of its problem-solving task, much of the important data necessary to a sound solution emerges in this process and this facilitates and accelerates the remaining steps. The steps shown in the figure are not mechanistic but interactive. Each depends for its soundness on the team member and teamwork skills. If the problem is highly technical, for example, and the 'boffin' with the real knowledge required is reserved and not much respected or encouraged by the 'activists', it is probable that the best solution will never be reached.

Then comes decision time. In my experience, when a team has worked together through an important issue in this way, the best choice of possible alternatives stands out clearly in most cases so there is agreement. In a sense the decision makes itself. However agreement is not always possible in the time available. Sometimes only one team member remains genuinely unconvinced by the advocacy of others, sometimes more than one. In these circumstances, teamwork does not resort to voting or majority rule. The decision must be made by the person in the team who is accountable. In so doing, that person is not obliged to make the decision in favour of the option for which he or she has argued most strongly. It remains possible for a team leader, for example, to make the decision in favour of the position advocated by a colleague where that colleague has clearly the longest suit in knowledge and experience relevant to the particular issue.

Participation and contribution mean that all team members understand the issues and the thinking. The presence of mutual trust, respect, confidence and support (characteristics of teamwork) makes team consensus possible as the best alternative to team agreement. **Consensus is the act of the unconvinced or not yet convinced team members giving wholehearted support and commitment to the implementation of the decision which has been made.**

Open to learn

Most people are slow learners. This arises in part because of our reluctance to face up and change the way we work and the discomfort of the 'growing pains' which usually accompany such change. But it is also due in part to our haphazard way of learning by much trial and frequent error, and to our lack of awareness of what can be learned through everything we do. When people work together, the tendency towards slow learning is multiplied.

This circumstance can be changed. It won't change itself and requires intervention which confronts the lack of awareness and the ad hoc nature of trial and error. Actions taken must increase awareness, stimulate alertness and foster anticipation: for example, awareness of what is actually taking place, listening and looking, attuned to niggling difficulties and new possibilities; alertness awakened by prompters and milestones, measures of progress and quality; anticipation of risk, of the unexpected, of the consequences of changes in people, techniques and the market place.

Awareness, alertness and anticipation tone-up and tune-up the mind so that 'critique' becomes a way of doing things for the individual, the team and the enterprise. Blake and Mouton explain this term in *Making Experience Work – the Grid Approach to Critique*:

> *Critique* is a term we can apply to learning directly from experience. Critique involves evaluating action in a thoughtful way before the action is taken, during the action, or when it has been completed. It is important because the test of planning is in the results achieved and their explanations which critique establishes. Better understanding of the cause-and-effect actions that result in solving a given problem through critique is thus the key to better planning for improved results in meeting similar problems in the future.

Critique is therefore systematic learning from experience. It is systematic because the user sets out to learn as an integrated part of doing. It is both art and discipline and the word is used in order to distinguish it from other words such as appraisal, evaluation, review which may or may not incorporate the depth and intentionality of critique. The art of critique is rooted in the desire to learn and uses the discipline of critique in ways which yield vitality, stimulation, enjoyment and satisfaction.

Critique is specific, not general. Critique is always *of* decisions, actions, results, methods, behaviour and processes *against* objectives, plans and standards. Therefore it is implicit that critique starts at the beginning of a task, project or operation. If objectives, plans and standards are absent, not specific or unclear, critique is not possible. The practice of critique is essential to accelerating learning and applying promptly what is learnt; it is at the heart of continuous improvement. Critique is to be practised by all those involved in any particular work experience. These experiences may be short-term or long-term, simple or complex. They may involve a person working alone, several persons working together or the whole team.

Consider the telephone as a simple example. If you are a person who spends significant time using the telephone, you could decide to study the way you do so in order to make some specific improvements. You could decide to do this over, say, a two-week period. You would be initiating a critique.

Remembering that critique is not just something you decide to do but is an examination of this action against some standard, you will also need to define, at least in your mind, what you consider important. Your standards might include such aspects as courtesy, friendliness, clarity of speech, making sure you understand and are understood, time taken, differentiating between very important and less important calls, as well as focusing on what you really want to achieve from the conversation. If you trade in your telephone for email, you will be able to apply your experience to this as well.

If you set your objectives and standards well, you can measure your progress from day to day. You can make some immediate improvements. Also, because you have been concentrating on getting better value from your time spent, you can modify, strengthen or add to the standards you have set. And you are now much more aware and alert so you will recognise traits you want to change and correct them on the spot. Then, if you want, you can experiment.

Critique is an important tool of experiment and innovation. Here plans may be tentative and objectives and standards uncertain to varying degrees. But being specific is not the same as being certain. The same conditions for critique therefore apply. The degree of tentativeness and uncertainty must be specified so that these characteristics are understood while the risks inherent and the measures taken to control risk are intelligently anticipated. From this, it becomes clear that critique is also at the heart of the innovative business which learns to experiment with acceptable risk.

The art and discipline of critique rely on all the skills of teamwork, but the presence of candour is essential. Candour itself grows out of courage and the strength of personal conviction; put together, we need enough courage of conviction (eg about doing things better) to over-come the apprehension and risk we may at first feel. Without candour there can be no critique.

This candour can be defined in two parts. Candour is feedback about what is observed. This feedback therefore describes the impact of observed actions on results, on how processes used worked to achieve the results and on the observed ways in which people contributed. It means putting all the cards on the table, telling it how it is or was seen. It is the means by which teams and enterprises learn to make facing-up a way of life.

Candour is also openness and frankness expressed in ways which are helpful. The description of what is actually taking place or took place illustrated with examples allows others to understand and accept what is said. It may sometimes be painful to hear but it is not spiteful or intended to hurt. It is incisive and focused but is not negative or personal criticism. Its purpose is to improve results and the ways in which they are achieved.

Candour of this kind does not stand alone. It takes time to emerge and the path is not linear. Trust must develop and team support must be given. Therefore the diagram on page 107 retains its relevance when the pathway is seen not as a straight line, but as a spiral or part of a spiral. A spiral provides the best diagrammatic portrayal of the inten-tional learning process.

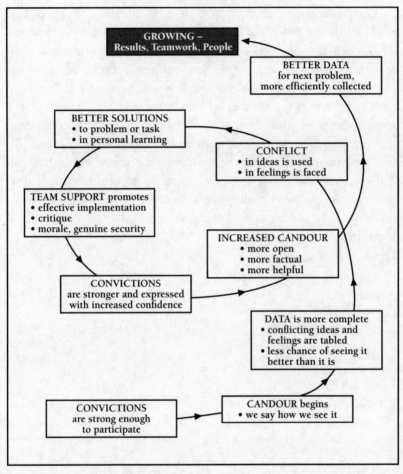

The intentional learning spiral for continuous
improvement in results, teamwork, people

The diagram above shows how the productivity of work teams, and the results achieved through the solutions produced by those teams, will improve as the team develops and practises its basic team skills to achieve genuine participation. People who work in teams in this way also grow and develop in confidence and competence so that personal development further advances team performance. Mutuality builds strength.

Growth and development in people, teams and enterprises that produces lasting benefits can almost always be represented and understood as a spiral experience. Just occasionally an individual or a business may appear to take a giant leap towards success. But for most successful businesses, or athletes to take another example, the achievement of growth, progress and success is much more like climbing a spiral staircase – building one step on another and repeating the cycle again and again, steadily gaining ground, height or skill.

I can't help thinking that there is something fundamentally true and lasting about this analogy. It even seems to be illustrated and confirmed in the discovery of the genetic database for life in all its forms – DNA, the helix of life's continuity. Even our origins have the form of a spiral!

Part 5

WHOLENESS

Openness towards Society

We acknowledge that excellence has the dimension of wholeness and that the pursuit of excellence brings obligations to recognise the interests of all who have a stake in the business, to act fairly, to practise integrity so that people can trust what we say, and to be a responsible member of society.

Chapter 17

A WIDER VIEW

I believe that caring for persons, the more able and the less able serving each other, is what makes a good society. Most caring was once person to person. Now much of it is mediated through institutions – often large, powerful, impersonal; not always competent; sometimes corrupt. If a better society is to be built, one more just and more caring and providing opportunity for people to grow, the most effective and economical way, while supportive of the social order, is to raise the performance as servant of as many institutions as possible by new voluntary regenerative forces initiated within them by committed individuals, *servants*. Such servants may never predominate or even be numerous; but their influence may form a leaven that makes possible a reasonably civilised society.

Robert K. Greenleaf's credo, from *On Becoming a Servant Leader*

Society is fickle. Risk is part of life and most certainly of business life. Memories are short.

At the beginning of the 1990s, in response to the business excesses (often encouraged by governments), greed, collapses and pain of the 1980s, there was a strong surge of advocacy for a renewal of business ethics. The writings of American corporate executive and educator Robert Greenleaf suddenly became fashionable. Greenleaf's best-known book, *Servant Leadership*, originally published in 1977, reappeared in all the best bookshops and on the 'must-read' lists of institutes of management, directors and business education. Previously unpublished material held by the Greenleaf Centre for Servant–Leadership appeared for the first time, for example the essays and addresses presented in *On Becoming a Servant Leader*. Concurrently, the coming of a new era of 'stakeholder capitalism' was heralded in numerous business journals.

Yet as I come to write this chapter, I feel a dilemma and a difficulty. The company I helped to build has recently gone through a rough patch. Part of the cause probably reflects a repetition of familiar leadership omissions where ambition and confidence to undertake contracts of any size ran ahead of a matching depth of experienced people (another reminder that, like liberty, the price of business survival and success is eternal vigilance). The larger scene is just as confusing and contrary. The juggernaut of the world economy rolls on. The Asian financial meltdown has come but not quite passed; financial markets seem to have weathered another cycle of nervous volatility and have entered an upbeat phase on the strength of new-technology stocks; and global mergers are producing giant enterprises whose activities dwarf the ecomonies of smaller nations. Pressure from investors, including superannuation funds and other large institutional investors, for short-term financial returns has not diminished, which contrasts sharply with continuing and sometimes righteously strident calls for a fairer, broader corporate perspective.

In these circumstances, a question constantly recurrs. Are the words from the Baulderstone Philosophy which introduce Part 5 an authentic, responsible, and practical aspiration for corporate behaviour, or are they little more than a dream motivated by another kind of self-indulgence?

To counter this moment of self-doubt, I turned to Robert Greenleaf, enlisting, perhaps conscripting, his credo by including it at the beginning of this chapter. Greenleaf challenges us with another question. Are institutions (including business enterprises) inescapably part of the society or societies in which they operate? Do John Donne's words 'No man is an Island, entire of itself; every man is a piece of the Continent, a part of the main' also apply to individual businesses? The move towards the globalisation of business does not dilute the question, although it is possible to think that it might. It should rather concentrate the minds of business leaders so they recognise that, by choosing to become larger, stronger and more influential, they automatically assume an increasing measure of the responsibility for maintaining or undermining a civil society.

In spite of times of questioning, I have remained persuaded that no business is an island and a business is more than the return it makes to its shareholders. The trend of market demand towards quality has strengthened this conviction. As I said in chapter two, there is a wide consensus that excellence, quality and service are to be the hallmarks of products and businesses of the future. If we purchase a high quality motor car we expect it to be without flaws, that it will last. Enterprises which are able to deliver sustained high quality will require congruent values to nourish their strategies, systems, processes and relationships. To believe otherwise is simply to place trust in false hopes. To put it another way, sustained quality demands a wider view than pure self-interest.

When they looked at the record of profitability, of visionary companies, James Collins and Jerry Porras came to a similar conclusion. In *Built to Last* they reported:

> Contrary to business school doctrine, we did not find 'maximizing shareholder wealth' or 'profit maximization' as the dominant driving force or primary objective through the history of most of the visionary companies.

and concluded:

> PROFITABILITY is a necessary condition for existence and a means to more important ends, but it is not the end in itself for many of the visionary companies. Profit is like oxygen, food, water and blood for the body; they are not the *point* of life but without them there is no life.

This they wrote about a group of companies which attained, on average, long-term financial returns to their stockholders 15 times greater than that for the general market, and six times greater than for the 'next-best' group of companies included in their study. It is a considerable comfort that they also identify 'resilience', not 'perfect, unblemished records' as a core characteristic: 'visionary companies display a remarkable resilience, an ability to bounce back from adversity.'

The specific words about profit in the first writing of the Baulderstone Philosophy were conceived through just such a time of struggle and adversity. The second writing came after a period of sustained and strong profitability. A wider view does not exclude the rigorous disciplines of financial performance. Giving attention to fairness, integrity and citizenship will support its consistent achievement – like a blue-chip stock, it yields high dividends over the long term.

Chapter 18

FAIRNESS

What is fairness?

Fairness grows out of respect and mutual interest. But how fair is fair? And who is the arbiter of fairness? From whose point of view is fairness to be judged?

Questions can be endless. Life and business experience conclusively demonstrate that events will never be perfectly fair, so it becomes all too easy to argue that fairness is just a matter of opinion. In this case argument seems to lead nowhere, leaving a simple choice. Will an enterprise take seriously its intention to act fairly by promoting it as a factor to be considered in all its acts and decisions? Or will the enterprise decide that aggressive self-interest, not fairness, is the dominant criterion and it is acceptable to screw every ounce of self-interest from every situation?

Fairness towards shareholders and employees

The table on pages 74–5 includes justice as one of the musts for motivation – my people know they will be treated fairly. Teamwork promotes fairness because it starts with mutual respect. Without respect teamwork is not possible. Teamwork enhances respect by valuing contributions and encouraging openness, listening, candour, facing-up, support for personal development, and promotion. It also provides feedback which includes commendation and recognition. It promotes a culture of problem-solving rather than sheeting home blame.

It is possible, though not necessarily easy, to treat every employee in these ways. Sometimes there are barriers which prevent an employer doing what he or she thinks to be fair. Take, for example, a situation where wages are strongly controlled by awards and a unionised work-force. A few years after I joined Baulderstone, I recall telling Bert that I wanted to recognise some of the best tradesmen and labourers who clearly contributed and produced more than others. Since promotion to leading-hand was neither being sought nor considered justified, my proposal was to pay these few employees more than the award. Bert's response was very definite: 'You can't do it. You'll have a dispute on your hands and then everyone will be discontented, including those you want to reward. They won't keep it to themselves – it will be common lunch-shed gossip. Then everyone will want it.'

Other aspects of fairness arise when an enterprise thinks about incentives. For an enterprise to share rewards between shareholders and employees is congruent with the 'stakeholder' principle – this is also in the longer-term interests of shareholders. Shareholders are entitled to a fair return on their investment consistent with the risks involved, in the same way that employees are entitled to fair salary or wages in return for their labour. When the level of profitability exceeds that which provides the shareholder with a fair return and a prudent re-investment in the business which is to the benefit of both shareholders and employees, there is the opportunity to pay an incentive. But who should receive it? And how much? And what form should it take – cash, shares, extra superannuation?

I have not yet found a perfect incentive scheme. Persuasive answers can be mounted for alternative responses to the questions just posed. Sometimes it has seemed that it is almost too difficult to design a scheme which is practical and seen to be fair, and which does not defeat its objectives by creating dissatisfaction.

Take bonus schemes as an example. The argument in favour of schemes with limited participation, put simply, says that only executive managers and some strategically placed operating managers (eg the head of a major project or production unit) are in a position to influence the level of profitability materially. The bonus pool (the total monies available for distribution) is always limited, and widening participation restricts the ability to reward outstanding performance as substantially as might otherwise be possible, and this in turn limits its impact on motivation. As well, it is only possible to assess individual contribution reasonably fairly and consistently for a small number of staff.

An option at the other end of the scale is to pay a general bonus in which every employee participates in proportion to his or her level of remuneration. Remuneration is adopted as a reasonable measure of comparative contribution. In medium-sized to large organisations, the inclusion of all employees significantly limits the size of the bonus paid to any person; perhaps the equivalent of one, two or three weeks pay will be possible. Two arguments put forward against this approach are that the bonus is not large enough to make a noticeable impact on the employee's living over and above the level of salary or wages paid, and that, because it is not tied to assessed individual performance during the particular period for which the bonus is paid, there is the risk that it will be seen as a hand-out, become expected and turn into a dis-incentive in periods when profit levels do not permit a bonus to be paid.

While these arguments have some force, it is also true that they arise out of a sceptical, even cynical, view of human nature. Put bluntly, it sees most employees as only interested in money – as not really inter-ested in the enterprise and impossible to educate anyway. If an enter-prise thinks this way, it has already disqualified itself, perhaps intentionally, from effective participation and teamwork development. Under these conditions, a general bonus will almost certainly be viewed in the way expected.

Paying a general bonus makes most sense when it is part of an inclusive work culture focused on the achievement of high standards of performance. An age-old question makes the essential point: who makes the music, the organist or the organ grinder? To have a bonus scheme which rewards *only* the most highly paid in an enterprise which is seeking exceptional performance through willing involve-ment is a contradiction.

The decision about whether to have a scheme at all remains diffi-cult. It is easy to conclude that the fairest course is simply to pay employees generously. But an individual enterprise doesn't operate in a vacuum and is always subject to market pressures and practices in remuneration. Employees can be attracted to and away from any enterprise, experienced people are always in short supply, and industry trends have moved towards performance-based rewards, particularly for senior appointments. In the end, the decision will only be sound if it fits and supports the ethos, values and goals of the enterprise. Experience has strengthened my own conviction that it is worth the effort to establish a scheme which includes both a general bonus element and the capacity to reward exceptional individual contribution. Apart from anything else, it does help keep in front of the whole enterprise the necessity and discipline of profitable operations.

This discussion has alluded to the subject of executive remuneration, which includes that of the chief executive. During the 1980s and 1990s in Australia, the remuneration of some chief executives escalated rapidly to levels previously unheard of in this country, motivated by the euphoria and the 'captains of industry' phenomenon of the eighties and the impact of international influences towards globalisation in the nineties. To build an excellent organisation requires leadership to match, and this is a scarce talent in a competitive market. But to build an excellent organisation which achieves quality performance through teamwork requires leadership which sees the enterprise as a whole. If the values on which an enterprise is founded and operates are not to be undermined, these competing forces must be held in a constructive tension which can be accepted (even if with some difficulty) by those who make up the enterprise as fair and reasonable given the market environment in which the enterprise has to operate. Such a constructive tension rules out the extremes.

An important corollary to this conclusion is that the board of directors of such an enterprise will in most cases have failed in its duty of care in respect of executive development and succession planning if it is forced to recruit a chief executive from outside the enterprise. The need to preserve core values and culture, but ensure these are kept alive and growing through the stimulation and challenge of competent people with different backgrounds and experiences, requires this enterprise to recruit potential leaders for other than the top job.

Partnering – building trust in the market place

The market place is a competitive arena. Fairness should therefore not be confused with softness. There is a sense in which the challenge, 'If you can't stand the heat, get out of the kitchen', is the reality. But then, not all good chefs are bullies.

The term 'partnering' became fashionable in the 1990s; it means moving towards a relationship of equals. In construction projects, this kind of relationship between a customer, design consultants and the contractor was much resisted in the 1960s and 1970s. Status barriers and predominantly adversarial stances round the formal contract prevented sensible problem-solving and caused much otherwise avoidable tension, delay to the project and paper warfare. As buildings became more complex (eg hospitals, laboratories, high-tech) and higher standards were imposed by governments and professions to cover the increased range of specialist structural, mechanical, electrical and electronic services and systems, a more cooperative approach slowly began to be considered.

In 1977 the South Australian Government experimented with a different approach to building the first of a series of colleges for technical and further education. Baulderstone was appointed to participate in the first of these projects in what was then a new role called construction manager. Responsibilities were firstly to contribute a constructor's know-how to planning and design proposals as a peer member with other consultants, and then to manage the construction phase, the actual physical works being done by trade or subcontractors.

The benefits we were by this time beginning to realise from investment in team-building had strengthened the conviction that this approach could result in better performance of the total project, not just the construction part. We also knew from experience that, while the concept of construction management was premised on the parties 'working together as a team', teamwork would not just happen. But we believed that if we could help make it happen, it would not only benefit the project but we could also gain an edge in what might become an important new niche market.

Being only one amongst equals (and probably still viewed by some as the least amongst equals) we tentatively suggested to the government's project director the idea of involving the team of professionals (client department, project manager, architect, structural engineer, mechanical/electrical engineer, quantity surveyor, construction manager) in some team-building and offered to conduct an exploratory training session for this team. The 20 people involved agreed, in spite of reservations and some reluctance, to participate in a two-and-a-half hour session. Feedback afterwards was more favourable than unfavourable, and participants expressed a willingness to engage in a further eight-hour workshop. Here project team members, working in four cross-disciplinary workshop teams, would seek to reach agreement on performance objectives, mutual expectations of team members (ie common performance standards for such elements as information transfer, timeliness and resolving differences) and improvement tasks. Even though benefits would have been greater if the workshop had occurred at the commencement of the project rather than six months in, the most tangible measure of the value of these two brief activities is that the project achieved all its important goals in terms of quality, cost and time without serious disagreements or conflict.

This pilot experience was a catalyst which helped Baulderstone become a leader in the construction management market. It became common practice to conduct team-building workshops at the commencement of most large projects irrespective of the form of contract, so that what had started in a small niche market with potential became a vehicle for accelerating the growth and development of people across the company. In this way it became a significant contributor to profitability and reputation.

Reaching agreement on objectives and standards in a multi-disciplinary team drawn from a number of participating enterprises is an activity which establishes fairness as a mark of team behaviour. The parties agree to what is expected in practical terms not just contractual terms; more cards are turned face up on the table. It brings about an increase in openness because difficulties created by any party or from any cause can be confronted and compared with what has been agreed. Therefore it promotes problem-solving over the taking of entrenched adversarial positions.

By the 1990s changes in the delivery methods of major construction projects (such as developer-initiated; design, construct and finance; the privatisation of community infrastructure development; and including projects undertaken through consortia and joint ventures) presented many more opportunities for genuine partnering approaches of this kind. While formal contracts remain necessary to define the obligations of the parties and how unresolved disputes will ultimately be determined, selection of partners places strong emphasis on participants who, in addition to the essential technical or commercial competence, have the people and reputation for resolving problems and contentious issues in a fair and reasonable manner without recourse to excessive claims and legal disputation. This trend is an example of choosing fairness with a strong element of self-interest. The market place, however, would be wise to be vigilant. As the term 'partnering' becomes more commonplace and trends towards overuse, the risk increases of assuming that careful selection of partners will ensure teamwork. Though this is an essential first step, it is not enough. **Teamwork never just happens.**

In a fiercely competitive market place, the relationship between a head contractor and its subcontractors and suppliers is a trading situation with a harder edge. The opportunity to act the bully is ever present, particularly by the head contractor, but sometimes also by the subcontractor when circumstances such as scarce resources give it the advantage. What should a head contractor do, to choose an example, when a subcontractor gets into financial difficulty? How hard should the game be played? No generalised answer can be given, for every situation will be different with causes reflecting varying degrees of competence, neglect and responsibility; neither does the question suggest a welfare obligation.

But the principle stands: sustained quality demands a wider view than pure self-interest. That wider view includes, in a case such as is presented here, the ability to stand where the other party stands, and to take this into consideration before deciding action. In this unpredictable world the circumstances might one day be reversed, even one day soon. Taking the harshest decision will sometimes be the right choice, sometimes unavoidable even if deeply regretted, and will almost certainly be seen as unfair by the other party. Every time, however, that any decision is taken as the act of a bully who for the time being has the upper hand, it is a flaw in the behaviour of the enterprise which diminishes its people and its capacity to deliver quality work or service.

Chapter 19

INTEGRITY AND
CITIZENSHIP

What is integrity?

Two teenage experiences give different pictures of integrity.

During my youth, a church leader talked to our boys' club about his life in industry. I cannot remember what his subject was on that occasion, but I do remember him using the illustration of employees taking home pencils and paper clips to make the point that honesty is honesty and small dishonest acts are just as important to integrity as more notorious ones. I sometimes wonder why this made a lasting impression.

Fifty years on, our grand-daughter Joanna had not long obtained her 'P' plates. She could use the family car but was not permitted to take friends with her until she had a year's experience. At the same time there was a mutual expectation that she would tell her parents where she would be. At a party one weekend, friends urged her to go to another venue. 'Your parents won't know', they said. Her response: 'No, they wouldn't. But I will know'.

While petty pilfering is to be discouraged, the essence of integrity is to ring true. The word relates to integer and integral, oneness and wholeness. It is the ability to keep in mind a picture of the whole while living in and working on the part. This is also a wider view that promotes quality.

Rules and codes

If striving for openness within the enterprise is a valid contribution to achieving high standards of performance, it is at the same time the best way to promote and preserve ethical business conduct. Having rules and codes can so easily become the end of action and a token commitment – we've proclaimed it, therefore it is. Consequently, I have come to favour maximum openness and minimum rules. A definition of fraud as 'the use of *deceit* to obtain advantage or to avoid an obligation' supports this view. The most deceitful will always be able to find a way around the strictest rules, but it is more difficult to hide in an enterprise that values openness.

Some simply stated rules are desirable for education and guidance to employees to make explicit what is expected in regard to such matters as gifts and favours, personal use of company purchase orders, misappropriation of company equipment and property, disclosure of commissions and discounts which belong to a customer, and misleading statements and returns to public authorities as are important and relevant to the business of the enterprise. Rules are supported by the disciplines of written procedures, of which one of the most important is the requirement that two persons approve financial transactions. An enterprise which promotes openness, including the standing invitation that any employee can approach (speak with, write to) any senior officer or director to discuss any issue of serious concern, significantly increases the difficulty of two employees conspiring successfully to beat the system.

Internal audit

Internal audit is one vehicle which is being used increasingly to strengthen the disciplines contained in proven practices and procedures. Where there is an adequate presence of openness and trust, the role and application of internal audit can be expanded constructively and an illustration from Baulderstone's experience explains one such undertaking.

At the start, possible barriers need to be acknowledged. The term audit carries for most employees the stigma of a policeman-type role, of checking up on employees which, by implication, includes checking for errors, misdemeanours and abuse. A further barrier is the caricature of the auditor as a nit-picker, someone who makes life more difficult for those who are the performers, the movers, shakers and profit-makers.

Baulderstone did not have a formal internal audit function before 1990. However, growth and geographical spread of the business with increased numbers of new people joining the company meant that a change was warranted. Even so, there was a strong desire to avoid the negative characteristics just referred to and to prevent this function inhibiting openness rather than supporting it. The problem was addressed on two fronts – what would be done and who would do it?

What did this company need from internal audit? It was a construction contractor carrying out projects with varying degrees of complexity and risk at dispersed locations. The major business risks for such an enterprise are project risks, essentially design and technical (eg conception, financing, planning, estimating, time, execution) and commercial (eg head contract, subcontracts, insurance, purchasing, financial and commercial administration).

Project conception, design and pricing expertise comprise the driving force of the business. Project execution and commercial expertise are the activities which keep that force under control. The greatest risks from concept, design and pricing causes occur right at the beginning of a project opportunity – at the time of conceiving, estimating and winning the work against competition. Controlling these risks depends mostly on the experience and judgement of the company's top leadership and senior line managers within a discipline of built-in checkpoints for objective critique. It was not considered that internal audit could add real value in this area over and above the criteria and disciplines set by the board.

For the project execution and commercial functions it was different. The company had developed and continued to upgrade its practices, procedures and computer-based control systems over a long period, often from hard-learned experience, so that it had confidence that, correctly applied, they were sound tools for maintaining control over the contractual and financial progress, obligations and needs of projects. Provided employees understood and followed these disciplines, they would produce accurate information and reports necessary to support sound decisions throughout the life of the project. It was therefore decided that the new internal audit activities would concentrate on these processes in a way that would increase value and provide service.

The challenge given to the audit committee by the board was to carry out these process audits in a way that contributed to an environment where:

- the board can have a high level of confidence in the financial forecasts presented to it
- activities are performed in the defined way and consistent with company values
- systems facilitate rather than frustrate the manager's ability to manage
- disciplines and procedures exist
- confidentiality, accountability and honesty are valued and practised
- opportunities exist for adding value through a process of quality improvement
- early warning signals provide management with the ability to respond quickly and effectively to issues.

To meet this challenge it would be necessary that internal audit be seen by those being audited (ie the staff on projects and in operating divisions) as a valued service not a burdensome imposition. Its dominant characteristics would be support, contribution, education and coaching, not policing. Choosing the auditor was therefore perhaps even more important than deciding what would be done, and this proved to be so. The company appointed as its first internal auditor its longest-serving, most experienced commercial manager, who had been looking for a new challenge with which to conclude his working life. His competence, unquestionable trustworthiness and the respect in which he was held resulted in the broadened goals of internal audit being consistently pursued and real improvement in the standards of project administration being achieved.

The exit meetings with project and division staff at the conclusion of each audit provided opportunities for strengthening understanding about why tasks were done in certain ways and about the ethos of the company for new employees, and for demonstrating by example the value of openness as a way of getting problems on the table, taking corrective action, improving results and systems, and preventing fraud.

When employees work in an environment where they do not have to keep looking over their shoulders to protect their backs, they are free to devote their undivided talents to productive effort.

Business conduct

Here is a lesson from tin cans. When we say we will open a can of tomato juice, we generally mean we will make two small holes in the top of the can. If it is a can of tomatoes, it is likely that we will cut the top of the can right off. Though each can is open, they are not open to the same extent. Openness is measured by what is needed – food or drink.

Internally, an enterprise which invites participation must also learn to distinguish between what individual employees and groups of employees need to know (for performance and commitment) and what some may want to know (for general interest or gossip). Sharing unnecessary information blocks channels, causes confusion, disperses focus and wastes time, all difficulties Baulderstone experienced when it started down the participative path in the early 1970s. Meetings are particularly prone to these kinds of temptation and misuse, sometimes abuse. Therefore, learning to get real value from fewer, shorter meetings by giving close attention to who participates and making sure they are properly prepared, planning and critique is a critical supporting competence in an effective enterprise. These are general requirements for an openness which works.

A different, though related, matter is that of openness and confidentiality. Confidentiality is an important and necessary constraint within every enterprise for sensitive business and personal information. It is more necessary and more sensitive when dealing with those outside where, for example, the enterprise must preserve its competitive position, its negotiating strategies and the privacy of partners and associates. This is the sphere of business ethics, a testing ground for integrity, of an enterprise being true to itself.

I do not think that grand words (in the form of codes of ethics or conduct) are much help to an enterprise, and have wrestled with whether it is possible to say anything which can be legitimate, sincere and practical on the subject of ethics. In the end, I determined that I would encourage all of us at Baulderstone to conduct our affairs under two standards against which we were prepared to judge our actions and have them judged.

The first, 'to act fairly', has been discussed. The second was 'to practise integrity so that people can trust what we say'. There is more integrity in a rogue who makes no secret of the fact that when he trades with you he'll take everything he can get than in the gentleman who is both smiling and devious. The rogue is true to himself. I have not encountered a business situation where this simple standard did not provide a practical guide to consistent behaviour. Which is not to say that we always measured up or that application is as simple as the standard. It is possible to deceive by giving part and withholding part of the information; but it is also possible to say in many situations, 'I can't tell you.' So it comes back to the intention and the reputation of the enterprise. If the enterprise means to be straight with those with whom it deals, to be on the level, and if it has a reputation for behaving in such a way, then the idiosyncrasies, inconsistencies and grey areas that are inevitably present in many situations will mostly be accepted.

In the end, integrity always returns to being true to oneself. We know whether we have tried to be fair, to stand where the other was standing in any transaction. We know if we have been straight with the other party.

Citizenship

Why corporate citizenship? The investors create the enterprise which provides employment and products or services to the community. The enterprise pays its taxes and contributes to the community again. So it's a legitimate question. Or is it?

Why individual citizenship? I work hard. I pay my taxes. Why should I do more? What more should be asked, expected? The questions are just as legitimate.

Simply to pose such questions, and they are posed, seems to beg the issue. For it is axiomatic – without citizenship, no democracy, certainly no civil society. And to repeat what was said before: choosing to pursue the globalisation of business or promoting privatisation of former government activities and enterprises increases the role and responsibility of business enterprises to contribute intentionally to maintaining a civil society.

The individual citizen makes his or her most lasting contribution to the community primarily through the person he or she is and how this influences actions and behaviour. Who a person is pervades every part of living; it is how life is lived as child, parent, friend, leader, mentor, educator, employer, employee … with all the rippling consequences from those points of influence. Citizenship remains an expression of character first before it is transmitted into actions.

In a similar way, an enterprise will make its greatest impact on the life of the community by the way it conducts its business. Every day its influences add to or detract from 'community capital' through its dealings with employees, customers, associates, traders and government. Respect for the whole and the other is at the heart of building community, just as it is the precondition for fostering willing employee involvement.

When an enterprise chooses to build its own future through developing its people by increasing their skills and knowledge of how to work together more effectively, and constantly challenging them to deliver and keep on improving quality services and products, and when it seeks fairness as well as firmness in all its business dealings, the ripples again spread out into the community through every point of contact. Whatever other ways an enterprise chooses to express its corporate citizenship (eg scholarships, sponsorships, philanthropy, community initiatives), this will remain its greatest contribution.

I can testify from personal experience that what I learnt at Baulderstone helped improve the level and quality of communication at home. There was room for improvement! But finding practical, let alone creative, solutions to the competing concerns for the company and the family continued to be a struggle. I know that this was a real difficulty for other members of staff, particularly project managers, general superintendents and foremen where the nature of the work and the industry imposed heavy demands and sometimes excessively long hours and absences from home. Even now, the lingering feelings of disappointment remain that we did not find ways of being more supportive to these employees. The challenge is still there and perhaps others will do better in the future.

Through an active corporate citizenship an enterprise continues to demonstrate mutuality and generosity of spirit with and to its employees. Enterprise and employee stand together in responsible membership of society. Sharing this wider view has the capacity to increase identification and strengthen motivation and commitment.

Part 6

JOURNEYING

Openness towards Ourselves

*Finally, arrogance has no place in the pursuit of
excellence, whereas legitimate pride in achievement and
genuine humility support it. We accept the challenge as
worthy though the goal remains beyond our reach even
as we make progress towards it. This reminds us that
we never know it all and learn from every experience.*

Chapter 20

A PERSONAL VIEW

Facing-up in leadership

Towards the end of the 1980s Baulderstone added two important words to its policy document. 'Leadership example' was made explicit as a necessary obligation in earning the commitment of employees to the company's values, aspirations, performance standards and pursuit of excellence – a reminder to leaders and a declaration to all that credibility demands internal consistency.

These two words confirm what is self-evident, but again there is value in being reminded. The executive group, and the chief executive in particular, cannot avoid – whether by intention or default – being the chief educators of those who work in their enterprise. Their example will either strengthen or undermine the integrity and soundness of the enterprise.

Advocating a spirit of openness and fostering its evolution throughout the enterprise inevitably commits leaders to a personal journey which can be described as 'openness towards ourselves'. That is the kind of learning about which it is not possible to write objectively; it is only possible to tell parts of the story.

Horizons of excellence

The significance of making a journey is to be found more in progress than arrival – passing milestones, entering new territory, facing the unfamiliar, absorbing experience. To embark on a journey towards excellence in any sphere is to accept that it is a journey with no possibility of arrival. Two experiences from the world of art and entertainment convey this idea dramatically.

I was privileged in 1984 to see an exhibition of ice-skating by a cast which included national and international stars. The level of talent was exciting and the audience enthusiastic. Then came Torvill and Dean. Everyone was spellbound. I had never previously seen any performance in which the free spirits of the individual partners had, through movement, music and emotion, merged to such a degree that we in the audience were conscious only of a single experience. While I might have described from my lack of knowledge and experience in skating the performance of the earlier stars as excellent, Torvill and Dean swept away this judgement by demonstrating that so much more was yet possible.

In her biography Ruth Cracknell, much-loved and celebrated elder stateswoman of Australian theatre, recounts an experience which was special to her, a performance of the ballet *Sleeping Beauty*, in London in 1954. After watching Margot Fonteyn (later Dame Margot) dancing at the height of her powers, she wrote a letter home which she quotes in her book *A Biased Memoir*:

> I can't analyse her dancing – I only know it is the most perfect thing I have ever witnessed, that it's ethereal, that it is light as swansdown, that it is fast as a whip crack, that it's a flower unfolding and growing before your eyes, that it's the most fragile, breathtaking thing I have ever seen – that, in short, it is magic . . . Never have I so wanted something to go on forever.

The dancing was perfect, beyond comprehension for Ruth Crackwell, but surely not for Margot Fonteyn. Only Margot Fonteyn, Jane Torvill and Christopher Dean would know how costly were these performances which appeared to the mere mortals in the audiences as so sublime. Only they would see how much improvement was still possible.

When I first started to play tennis at secondary school, I would watch with amazement and longing the talent of the members of the school's 'A' team. When I managed in later years to scrape into that team, I took every opportunity to see national tournaments, on one occasion a Davis Cup tie, and the possibilities for improvement stretched forth endlessly.

This recognition that as our competence develops in any activity so the boundaries of what we perceive as possible continually recede is a universal characteristic of every growing person and enterprise. As we climb the mountain, we can see further.

I have found this insight to be very important in the development of leadership which exhibits both depth and strength. It is one that was stressed at the end of the Baulderstone in-house Grid seminars which lasted five days and were conducted regularly after 1976 for all new employees in supervisory and technical positions.

Any seminar of this kind can only provide a first step forward if the subject has broken new ground for the participant (which includes new ground in the sense of the subject now being taken seriously). The danger then is that the participant will see the ultimate horizon through the eyes of a graduate from first grade. At the point when our employees were about to leave the cloistered environment of the seminars and return to the world of real life and work, I wanted to keep their feet firmly on the ground but their eyes pitched to take in the far horizon and not just the front gate.

We hoped that they had by this time caught a glimpse of the benefits that could flow from choosing teamwork. I also wanted them to see that it is possible to create and sustain those conditions which yield the enthusiastic, creative involvement of employees in achieving the goals and purpose of the company, that it required a long-term commitment from them as well as the company, and that as the pathway to building an excellent enterprise teamwork is a demanding, rewarding choice. So they were now invited to look at the way ahead for their own development and practice as managers through several sets of eyes, the eyes of managers A, B and C.

Manager A is proud of being a worldly-wise, hard-nosed business achiever. She is likely to view teamwork as a soft option, whereas a more valid understanding would come from looking at the contrast between brittle and tough. Manager B feels strongly about the welfare of the people in the enterprise and values harmony and a good feeling. He will frequently decide that, because of its challenging goals, standards, disciplines and expectations, teamwork looks too hard, too much facing-up, too harsh, but more valid conclusions might be seen in the contrasts between warmth and strength, sympathy and compassion.

Manager C has a different approach. She wants results but also has a genuine interest in her people. This manager knows best what is needed and knows that she knows. Suggestions are invited in group discussions, the manager decides, leads from the front, expects hard work and compliance, and rewards generously when the job is well done. Manager C cannot see the potential of a different level of participation beyond her own confident position. Hers is a façade of teamwork too easily arrived at, which tempts enthusiastic first-grade graduates to settle for excellence on the cheap if they believe they already know it all. My greatest reservation about some of the best-seller 'excellence' texts is that they point to an horizon too easily reached. What they prescribe and how to get there, while being helpful and useful, tends in my experience towards 'cheap excellence'.

In contrast, choosing teamwork as the way forward is 'costly excellence' (of the kind won by, for instance, Torvill and Dean and Margot Fonteyn). It seeks to generate morale and synergy that are quite different in nature, quality and impact from those expected by Manager C. On a small number of occasions, teams in which I have worked turned in dramatically better performances than was our norm. The talents of the team were multiplied, not just added together. These experiences, though few and infrequent, made such an impact that they were enough to convince me that the striving in this direction is worth it even if it takes a lifetime.

The depth, strength and toughness that are inherent qualities of winning teams (sporting or industry) are the source of Collins' and Porras' 'resilience' in visionary companies. As a consequence, teamwork has the potential to deliver satisfaction and fulfilment to the greatest number of people. Seeing and accepting that the scope for learning and growing is forever open-ended is living life with a spirit of hope and adventure.

Chapter 21

LESSONS FROM LIVING

Loneliness

A phrase from one of Swiss physician and author Dr Paul Tournier's many books sticks in my mind. 'There are no strong people; only strong reactions and weak reactions.' His 'strong reactions' could otherwise be described as being definite, forceful, certain, with no room for doubt. Over the years I have come to view such outward confidence as frequently papering-over a person's inner uncertainty.

It is true that learning, growing, experimenting and discovering are stimulating and satisfying. But they also sometimes bring feelings of loneliness and uncertainty, for the inward journey cannot be avoided if openness is valued. The pathway to openness runs both ways. In both directions it leads to places of facing-up. Openness is what it says – we learn to put the cards on the table and look at them face up.

I have described some of the situations in my work at Baulderstone that forced me to do this in spite of my predisposition to be a slow learner. These work experiences took me in the direction of that inward journey which brings us to face and accept who we really are – what we like about ourselves and what we would prefer not to see. After I had walked this way a few times, I was surprised and encouraged that facing-up did become easier – though I've always felt resistance!

It is a truism that leadership is sometimes lonely. Working to build an effective team acts as a buffer to the loneliness of leadership because team support is a condition of teamwork. I was fortunate from the early 1970s to have this kind of team support from my team members and other employees who were active colleagues. Nonetheless, I did not escape loneliness altogether and there were situations which tested personal conviction, imposed difficult choices and required the acceptance of disappointment.

When business was really tough, during one of the periodical recessions in the construction industry for example, or when a project was losing money, I sometimes wondered whether my notion of building an excellent company with a distinctive participative culture was no more than a pipe dream. Was it worth the effort? This was particularly so when I sensed, rightly or wrongly, that others might be asking a similar question. Yet I knew deep down that I believed in what we had set our hand to – and I had seen enough evidence of outstanding performance when we got it right and in real growth and development amongst employees to support this belief. When confronted with these contradictory thoughts and feelings, the leader of an enterprise, having faced honestly the presence and temptation of uncertainty, has only one course – to hang in and hang on to that inner conviction which is the well-spring of leadership example.

Quite recently I was talking with one of the company's best young project directors who had for more than a year been going through his most torrid and difficult project experience. I spoke with him just after he had seen a first glimmer of light at the end of the tunnel. Reflecting on his dark, lonely days, he said: 'Sometimes you just have to keep on doing what is right, believing that things will work out in the end.'

Such 'things' always need conviction and persistence in order to work out. The case of competing priorities or benefits provides another example. Good apples can turn sour. During the 1970s Baulderstone recruited a number of project managers from other parts of Australia. Two of these managers proved to be highly competent and the significant projects they headed turned in good results. Each brought a new breadth of larger project experience and practical knowledge to the relatively secluded market of a small State. The company's performance, capability and reputation benefited. Each had more to contribute and we sought to make this possible when their projects were completed.

The nature of construction breeds project managers who are and like to be kings of their castles. They may actively involve other project staff in thinking and planning, though often their approach follows more closely that of Manager C described in chapter 20. There was, however, another dimension in the cases cited. These new project managers turned into empire builders with a Machiavellian touch. They sought personal loyalty of staff in order to undermine company leadership. Regrettably there could then be no place for them.

My sorest test of leadership example came at a time when the company had entered a strong growth phase and the roles and membership of my team had changed in response to this development and its demands. Over a period, a deep-seated tension between several team members became a major barrier to the quality of our team action because of diminished respect, openness and trust. For a long time I lived with this situation because I couldn't see how to bring the issues to a head in a way which would bring about a constructive result for the company and these colleagues. The tensions were too volatile and the consequences of confrontation, I felt, were too unpredictable.

On the one hand each person was a highly valued, long-serving executive; I did not think it was in the company's interest to lose any of them, particularly at that time. On the other hand, the problem was not a secret and I know I was seen by some staff as too weak or too loyal to one or other for not dealing with it. I had been for many years, and still was then, the leading advocate for teamwork, team-building and a culture of openness and facing-up, and here I was being seen as unwilling to practise what I preached. I could not discuss my dilemma, because of its nature, with anyone in the company and I felt I was living a lie – the situation was lonely and deeply distressing.

Eventually, when I considered the tensions might be manageable, I arranged a face-to-face discussion in the team having first distributed to each a description of the problem as I saw it and a suggested procedure for starting the discussion. After that, the team began to work more cohesively again though the difficulties did not completely disappear. We are complex beings and do not live in a perfect world – or work in a perfect enterprise. Accepting this is not a reason to give up on the journey.

Humour

A sense of humour is probably the most important safeguard of humility.

When I was growing up I often felt admiration and envy toward people in our crowd who always seemed to be the life of the party. Looking back, I can see how some used their gift to hide insecurity and later rigidity. This gift of making others laugh, which can make a delightful contribution to a crowd or in a team, does not always reveal the sense of humour that safeguards humility.

A different experience comes from the early years of my married life when Judy and I lived in the newly established city of Elizabeth. Because there were few services or facilities, young families were thrown together in their common need to make their own community life and their own enjoyment. The enduring friendships we formed have been one of the great blessings in our lives. We were a mixed lot – rowdy, intensely shy and all shades in between. We remember our get-togethers mostly for their wall-to-wall laughter, often till it hurt. There was a wonderful sense of fun and the ridiculous to which everyone contributed, occasionally the quiet, dry ones most of all.

This is a better illustration of the sense of humour which is not dependent on personality, which keeps our feet on the ground and regularly reminds us not to take ourselves too seriously even when we are dealing with serious matters. Humility is strength which acknowledges both talents and foibles. We never know it all.

Time out

In another of his books Paul Tournier claims that:

> In meditation we see quite simple things in our lives which our intelligence has failed to perceive. We are also inspired to act; for true life is made up of an alternation between meditation and action. They are complementary: meditation leads to action, and action is matured in meditation.

And Dr Rollo May, internationally recognised psychiatrist, educator and author, adds a dimension to Tournier's observation in *The Courage to Create*:

> . . . creative insights of all sorts come to us in moments of relaxation. They come not haphazardly, however, but come only in those areas in which we are intensely committed and on which we concentrate in our waking, conscious experience.

During my student years, I frequently wrestled with some maths or science problem long into the night before giving up in frustration – only to find that the solution fell out in minutes in the morning, as clear as the new day.

Tournier and May, who are respected practitioners and observers in the field of health, summon those in leadership and positions of responsibility to consider this most neglected resource, inexpensive and available to all. Whether we prefer to call it meditation, contemplation, reflective thought or prayer, and whether we choose to make time for it under the shower or in the park or the study, the basic conditions are the same, solitude and quiet. For me, it was early morning before the household stirred. I jealously guarded this time and know how often it was my salvation.

Nurturing

Robert Greenleaf, on whose experience and wisdom I have drawn a number of times, was his own person. He had a gift for leadership but deliberately chose not to become a leader–manager because he did not see himself cut out for that. His interest in organisations and enterprises was first awakened by a wise, rather than brilliant or exciting professor who gained his attention with these words:

> There is a 'people problem' in all modern institutions, particularly in American business. It is a problem of how to lead the enterprise, particularly the larger ones, so as to elicit the best effort and provide the most satisfying existence to the people who work there. Some of you ought to get inside these institutions and work on this

problem. Outside, you can write, preach, research, advocate, and legislate. But if you really want to do something about it, you have to get inside, establish yourself, and commit yourself in a way that makes it possible for you to be influential.

He made this advice his own and later told a university audience:

I am primarily a doer, not a scholar. I have been more interested in wielding influence than in abstract thought. I chose to get inside the institution, accept enough of its ways to survive in it, and work on the problem rather than stay outside and write, think, teach, or advocate. I had enough of the organisation man in me to survive inside.

Greenleaf was once described by the president of his company, AT&T, as a 'kept revolutionary'. He could also be described as a nurturer, one who sees the possibilities, the direction, the light on the far hill, and keeps on pointing, nudging, castigating, encouraging, facilitating, explaining and binding up cuts and bruises.

Baulderstone's experience taught that three ingredients are necessary in establishing and then maintaining a participative enterprise.

First, there must be critical mass. Enough people must join the army in order to make progress against the 'old ways'. This is what Baulderstone achieved in the 1970s having failed in its first attempts in the 1960s.

Second, making progress requires action on a number of mutually reinforcing fronts. That is how I see the elements of the Baulderstone Philosophy which provide the subjects for the separate parts of this story.

Finally, what has begun to grow needs constantly to be nurtured by ongoing communication, teamwork (winning teams never stop practising) and critique. Nurtured also by individual employees who believe in the ethos of the business and take personal initiative to support and reinforce it. A garden which has taken many years of dedicated care to design and establish will be overgrown in a single season unless it is tended.

One of the sources of my greatest personal satisfaction and gratitude comes from knowing that I am able to name employees from every rank and part of Baulderstone who diligently nurtured the company's spirit and good name. Nothing of worth would have endured without them.

Part 7

TEAMWORK IN A NEW MILLENNIUM

The Versatility of Openness

The danger is not actual despotic control
but fragmentation—that is, a people increasingly
less capable of forming a common purpose and
carrying it out.

Charles Taylor, *The Ethics of Authenticity*

Chapter 22

MAKING A CHOICE — POWER OR PROBLEM-SOLVING

Whither the future – society

In his small book *The Ethics of Authenticity*, Charles Taylor confronts the helplessness a growing number of citizens in western society feel as we enter the new millennium. He names fragmentation as the signal danger arising from several modern malaises. He also says that 'our degrees of freedom are not zero'.

Building on these words of hope, he reaches a conclusion which points to a way forward:

> What our situation seems to call for is a complex, many-levelled struggle, intellectual, spiritual and political, in which the debates in the public arena interlink with those in a host of institutional settings . . .
>
> But to engage effectively in this many-faceted debate, one has to see what is great in the culture of modernity as well as what is shallow or dangerous.

Business enterprises, perhaps more than other institutions, have the talent, willingness and self-interest to look for what is great in present and emerging modernity. It is a characteristic ability which confirms Robert Greenleaf's observation that 'businesses are least lulled to complacency by idealistic pretensions and the support of sentiment'. In this setting, it also can be viewed as a working out of Peter Drucker's prophecy for one of the future roles of managers and enterprises:

> Management will increasingly be the discipline and the practice through which the 'humanities' will again acquire recognition, impact and relevance.

Drucker is challenging management to become a bulwark against fragmentation.

A complementary picture of our probable future is provided by Australian social researcher and writer, Hugh McKay, this time a collective community view. Insecurity, inherent instability, inconsistency, contradiction, ambiguity are the words he uses to describe the emerging social scene in the concluding pages of his recent book *Generations*, in which he explores and contrasts the attitudes, values and outlooks of the last three generations of contemporary Australians. He suggests:

> Knowing there is inherent instability in the process of social and cultural development, we could train ourselves to cope with inconsistency, contradiction and even ambiguity.

The problem is not going to go away so we should learn to face it.

Where to now – the market place

Another set of images or imaginings, this time for industry, can be assembled from phrases chosen more or less at random from reports and articles printed in recently published business journals.

For the market place:

> *Onslaught of global change; global economy brings new dimensions of competition; migrating capital, information, products and services have already become trans-national or non-national; digital media, information technology and telecommunications are driving world-wide economic and social change; global media are creating a mostly young customer class around international brand names; new sets of rules are being imposed by society and interest groups; increased public pressure for ethics, standards of conduct, accountability ...*

For the enterprise:

> *Far more complex, far more dynamic; networking, outsourcing, joint ventures, alliances; knowledge and knowledge workers are what matter; great number of autonomous contributors; minimise cost, maximise revenue; institutional or other investors have little or no loyalty to the enterprise; decreased loyalty of employees; decreased loyalty to employees; free agent takes over from organisation man; ethics, fairness, trust and vision matter more in environments which diminish tangibility of leadership skills; growing concentration of voting power in hands of institutional managers to elect/remove directors ...*

For leadership:

> *More flexible, creative thinking styles; imagination before memory; global perspective; personal insight, reflective practice; build in continuous learning; build networks rather than pyramids; creating, as well as managing, change brings risks of heavy toll – job tenure, stress, chronic fatigue, anger, self-criticism, cynicism; persuade rather than command; big-picture thinking; learn to share; create meaning and uphold values in flatter more dispersed structures ...*

There are, in addition, even more radical scenarios being seriously promoted, such as one that questions the ability of capitalism and business to cope at all with the social and ecological consequences of present trends.

Whatever picture gains our attention, one fact seems almost certain: enterprises, like people, to borrow Hugh McKay's words, will have to train themselves to cope with insecurity, inherent instability, inconsistency, contradiction and ambiguity – the many faces of fragmentation. Those people who cope best with uncertain circumstances know that, though these pressures may cause difficulty, discomfort and distress, they will survive for the very reason that the conditions are external – their internal strength and well-being does not depend on them. Therefore, they are also freer to look at their world with greater objectivity, creativity and adaptability in order to find the opportunities which are always present.

It is not too different for the successful, surviving enterprise. The more changes and unpredictability in the market place, the greater the need for internal strength and well-being. This explains why we find, amongst the scattered images (maybe longings would be more accurate) foreseen for the enterprise which will survive the future market place, such statements that ethics, fairness, trust and vision matter more in environments which diminish the tangibility of leadership skills. These qualities are the substance from which leaders will continue to create meaning and uphold values in flatter, more dispersed structures.

Combating fragmentation

Is it surprising that these words for tomorrow pick up one of the recurring themes of this story of yesterday – the theme of roots? I do not find it so. Working in the construction industry was a useful introduction to any turbulent, unpredictable market place. The following experience illustrates that this market has rarely been anything but fragmented.

In 1975 the national convention of the Australian Federation of Construction Contractors considered the issue 'Teamwork – Australia's Frozen Resource'. The productive capacity of the nation's infrastructure industry was locked in the grip of a stifling fragmentation depicted by the vast multitude of employer associations, awards, trade unions and industrial tribunals all pushing their own barrows. Added to this fragmentation, and destined to remain that way because of it, was the low priority given to the industry by government except for ad hoc pump-priming before elections. While I don't suggest that this environment parallels the changes facing enterprises at the start of the new millennium, it could certainly be described as inherently unstable, inconsistent, contradictory and ambiguous. The record of industry bankruptcies since then underlines its insecurity.

The convention may have raised the awareness of delegates and pointed to some constructive action to bring about improvements in industry performance and the individual enterprises within it, but there was not the common ground to generate the energy and commitment to make worthwhile change. Fifteen years later, the Federation itself was wound up. It had been unable to maintain sufficient common purpose, meaning and shared values.

Enterprises of the future face strong fragmenting pressures from factors such as size, global or international spread, employee turnover, employee loyalties, outsourcing and the moves towards operating through joint ventures and alliances. Phil Ruthven, one of Australia's most articulate industry forecasters, has been challenging the thinking of business and community leaders for years with social, economic and market trend lines from the huge data bank that his business assembled. In a conversation with Baulderstone's executives in 1989, his first piece of advice was 'be prepared to change or discard everything about your business except the values and beliefs on which it is founded'. He was talking about roots.

The chief executive cannot be everywhere to nurture the strong roots of the enterprise when it grows and migrates across boundaries and cultures, even though modern technology makes it easier for him or her to be seen everywhere. The leadership example of those senior colleagues close to the action will either support or fragment the message. Principles and actions of the kind discussed in Parts 2 and 3 of this book will help but there is a prerequisite. That prerequisite is illustrated by the understanding of delegation – one person cannot represent another as agent if he or she does not understand precisely what the delegator wants to achieve and how the delegated assignment fits into the delegator's overall thinking. And it is also illustrated by the enterprise's conviction about leadership succession – the need to preserve core values and culture, but ensure these are kept alive and growing through the stimulation and challenge of competent people with different backgrounds and experiences, requires this enterprise to recruit potential leaders for other than the top job.

Growing future leaders who share the dream and a commitment to the roots that sustain it is the most critical and difficult challenge facing the 'visionary company' because growing such future leaders takes time. For a medium-to-large enterprise leaders make up a significant number of people, so those experts who are predicting maximum terms of employment of not more than five to seven years as the norm for the future will have to revise upwards their forecast for this group or give away commitment to the foundations on which the enterprise stands, ie concede to the pressures of fragmentation. Recruitment will not reduce the time needed, for as learners and trusters we are yet still human. As a corollary, leadership development programs will have to include innovative ways of broadening the horizons, experience and strategic skills of these future leaders.

Operating an enterprise of the future with fewer direct employees, reduced employee loyalty, more free agents or contract employees, and through increased outsourcing, partnerships and alliances again invites all the potential risks, diversions and frustrations of fragmentation. If, therefore, the analogy presented in the figure on page 110 has merit, then tomorrow's enterprise will require an even more robust operating system. Yet the scene is not complete and other predictions might be added, such as predictions that knowledge and knowledge workers are what matter, and that successful enterprises will build networks not pyramids, persuade rather than command, build in continuous learning. As the insights, knowledge and experience needed for making the best decisions become more dispersed and diffuse as a result of these combined influences, both the case and the potential for teamwork and team action strengthens rather than weakens. Teamwork acts as an antidote to fragmentation.

The theme of teamwork in this story uses experience at Baulderstone to identify principles and practices that present ways of building strength through better solutions to whatever opportunities, problems, changes or conditions the enterprise anticipates or encounters. Baulderstone approached this challenge in one way and had some success. There are other ways, and hopefully more effective ways are emerging through experience, **but the principles, attitudes and skills of teamwork which overcomes fragmentation are enduring**.

Looking back or looking forward, I find reassurance in some ancient words attributed to Socrates by Plato:

I cannot repudiate my own words: the principles which I have hitherto honoured and revered I still honour, unless we can at once find other and better principles.

Testing the premise

Over the last decade I have observed, from the position of a non-executive director, the experiences of three diverse enterprises. The first two are examples of effective problem-solving, the third became trapped for years in an interminable power struggle.

A small business selling specialist equipment and services to the construction industry, and with an overseas parent, had been managed successfully for 30 years by the man who planted it in Australia. He knew the business intimately and managed it autocratically. Not surprisingly, there was not a future leader amongst his subordinates. As he approached retirement he was persuaded to recruit a successor and, in consultation with the chairman of the board, appointed a young executive seen to have the ability, but without experience in the enterprise's business or market. The chief executive (CEO) treated him like everyone else! So it was something of a miracle that he stayed for the three years he had to wait for his opportunity to take charge of the business.

Desiring to bring about a radical change in expectations, attitudes, accountability, communication and relationships, the new CEO gained the agreement of his mostly long-serving colleagues to a program of intensive teamwork development. After two years the impact was such that he was freed to concentrate his considerable energy and creative talent on the development of business and markets across south-east Asia, while the Australian business continued to prosper under the direction of his colleagues. In spite of an unexpected and unsettling change of ownership (through takeover of the parent), during this period the enterprise grew strongly and has consistently delivered outstanding financial returns.

The second experience comes from a very different field. According to knowledgeable overseas observers, Australia has a commendable aged-care infrastructure by world standards, particularly the services provided through the not-for-profit sector serving the middle-income and poorer members of the community. This sector had mostly been initiated by and grown through church or charitable organisations over a 50-year period. Part-way through that period, growth had been accelerated by greatly increased financial support from government for capital works and the underwriting of operational costs for recognised organisations through a system by which the government picked up any financial deficit suffered by an organisation. This system had remained unchanged for a long period and, as might be expected, had contributed to escalating costs, lax financial accountability, and a kind of easy comfortableness in providing a well-regarded service of care.

Then all this changed. For more than a decade, aged-care providers have been in turmoil as they learn to adapt to continual disruption imposed by erratic government decree on top of the growing demands of an ageing population. Government policy changed by declaring that the future priority would be to help ageing citizens remain at home. Some of the funds previously reserved for institutional care in the form of hostels and nursing homes would be redirected. Deficit financing ceased and was replaced by formula-based funding tied to numbers of residents and an assessment of their frailty. Providers were made wholly accountable for the financial control of operations, but the income-generating formulae have already changed a number of times. Government capital funding for new facilities and upgrading older facilities has largely ceased, replaced in part by resident loans. Concurrently, government introduced an onerous system of monitoring requiring higher standards of hostel and nursing home-care and buildings culminating in sudden-death accreditation requirements to take effect in the year 2000. Organisations will have to meet accreditation standards or get no operating funds – while the standards will progressively become more onerous over a further eight years.

One impact of these changes has been to decrease the number of hostel and nursing-home beds available. This will accentuate what is already happening as a result of a population that is growing older. Aged-care providers have watched the average age of residents in these facilities rise by ten years over a ten-year period. The increase in frailty and consequent health costs are starkly illustrated by the statistic that now more than half of all nursing-home patients suffer from some form of dementia or incontinence.

Overall, this is another set of circumstances which could rightly be described for the enterprises operating within them as insecure, unstable and ambiguous – another window, therefore, to the future.

The small not-for-profit institution of which I have close knowledge was ill-equipped to face these uncertain conditions following the retirement of a competent CEO at the start of the period of dramatic change. Several changes of leadership over the next few years at the CEO level and also director of nursing level accentuated internal instability which was marked by resentment, power struggles between health care and corporate managers, low morale and serious financial losses. The enterprise was starting to fragment from within.

The present CEO, an experienced, down-to-earth, open-minded health administrator, was appointed to fix the internal storms in order to face the hurricane brewing outside. After an initial period concentrating on matters of crisis and high urgency, he has steadily moved to embrace teamwork as a way of life for himself, his leadership colleagues and the whole institution. This small enterprise now has its house in order. It is amongst the best placed to achieve accreditation in advance of requirements, is growing its own leaders, has increased its quality of care and is gradually breaking down barriers inherited from the persistent hierarchical preferences of some health-care professionals. There is a new spirit in the place and it is consistently achieving strong financial surpluses which will provide the capital for future services.

A third experience has a less favourable outcome. A public utility of long standing with a good reputation operated as a somewhat independent corporation under its own board and enabling legislation. It had 6000 employees. Following the retirement of one CEO, the board selected a new CEO from the private sector, a person with strong leadership credentials and experience in large enterprises in several countries. It was the first time in the utility's 50-year history that any top leadership position had been filled from outside the enterprise.

The new leader inherited a high-cost operation at a time when all governments were under increased budget pressure to reduce costs and increase revenue, particularly contributions from State-owned corporations. In addition, he was anticipating the major upheaval to which this and other similar utilities would be subjected over the coming decade from the forces of privatisation and the opening of previously captive monopoly markets to competition. He believed he had about five years to dramatically change the culture of his enterprise to prepare it for these new conditions.

Because of the magnitude of this task and the restricted time he saw available, he gained the board's approval to invest very substantial sums to buy needed assistance and support in the form of specific services from the most experienced consulting practices. The challenge was to replace an inward-looking, largely bureaucratic operation in which decision-making was pushed upwards and concentrated in the top hierarchy (including the board) with a dynamic, market-oriented enterprise delivering competitive services through sound teamwork. He involved a wide cross-section of employees in analysing what needed to be done and establishing plans and targets, so gaining an important measure of commitment to stimulating though painful changes. These inevitably included facing up to a large reduction in the number of employees, a problem resulting from undisciplined over-staffing in the past.

In those five years, the workforce was reduced to 4000 without any serious disruption to operations and real achievements were made in improving the financial return. The contribution to government increased substantially. Many employees responded and grew in the new environment and contributed to creative innovations in work practices. Others struggled. The emerging enterprise's point of greatest vulnerability internally was the limited experience of its operating managers at all levels. Some were new to the responsibility, all were working in very different conditions from those to which they were accustomed. These managers, who had always operated with orders coming down from above, were now required to take initiative and be accountable. Rapid learning curves always include both success and failure, and some abuse. The negatives are sources of secondary confusion and reaction which also have to be dealt with.

Taking stock, it could be said that a highly promising start had been made in preparing the enterprise for the fast approaching, competitive market conditions, but it was only a start. The whole enterprise was fragile and it would take at least another five years of similar determination and commitment to build strength and stability into the new ways of doing things. There was more openness within the enterprise than five years earlier, but widespread trust was still to be earned.

Less progress had been made in establishing clearly articulated goals shared by the board and its sole government shareholder. Despite requests over several years, government declined to commit itself to agreed targets for return on investment, contributions to government revenue and reinvestment for development and replacement of infrastructure. Government therefore, while demanding greatly improved performance from its utility, failed to establish the financial criteria which would enable it to make its business plans with confidence. In this respect there was an absence of openness and, by implication, an absence of appropriate public accountability. For years, these decisions had been made with a sensitive finger testing the political wind.

When the chief executive decided not to renew his contract at the end of the five years described, it set off a chain of government interventions which determined the utility's future without effective consultation with the board. The value of the many millions of dollars invested in equipping the enterprise for the competitive market was either indiscriminately disregarded or heavily discounted and the benefits from all the effort neutralised. There has been no accounting of the huge financial cost. Neither can the human costs to employees, and through them to the community, from unnecessary distress, distrust, resentment and cynicism be measured. Where there had been emerging strength and value, there was now disenchantment and dissent.

Politicking in this sense, whether from without or within the enterprise, is the great destroyer of openness and trust. It makes teamwork impossible because it puts personal power before problem-solving. *My* solution, *my* way, *my* influence take precedence over the search for best solutions. Regrettably, I have encountered it too often in churches and their leadership and administrative committees when 'my beliefs' and 'my convictions' are so tightly held that openness cannot be tolerated. I have also encountered it in the councils of government planning, educational institutions and industry associations where self-interest and sectional interest dominate ahead of facing-up to the whole problem or issue in order to find a solution which best serves the purposes of the whole body.

The political approach comes in many subtle and aggressive forms of pressure, manipulation, threat, persuasion and even good intentions, but always with the same result – no openness, no trust, no teamwork, and poor solutions.

The enterprise as catalyst

Transparency mitigates fragmentation. A few of the very strong may prosper by a strategy of divide and conquer, but a civil society will not. Neither will most enterprises, for these require some civility in order to operate and survive. The enterprise which chooses greater transparency as a means of harnessing productive participation will be better equipped to succeed in the uncertain, fragmentary environment which is our future. This is my premise, that openness is versatile.

Paradoxically, through this pathway of considered self-interest the enterprise is also likely to make its greatest contribution to mutual interest. Sustained high-quality performance requires congruent values and relationships which cannot be fenced off. Quality and transparency practised within an enterprise spill over into the whole of life. In this way, the visionary enterprise with the wider view becomes inevitably, and even unconsciously, model and catalyst in Charles Taylor's 'many-levelled struggle' against fragmentation.

Part 8

REFLECTION

The Fruitfulness of Openness

My own humanity was awakened, rising up to greet me with a handshake as I watched the first glimmers of sunlight peak over the horizon. There's such a big difference between being dead and alive, I told myself, and the greatest gift that anyone can give anyone else is life.

James McBride, *The Colour of Water*

Chapter 23

FEET ON THE
GROUND

Success has more than one face

I am an advocate for openness. I seek to encourage others to choose it
as a core value in building corporate strength, a core contributor to survival and business success. I start and end this story with expressions
of my conviction that it works and that it will continue to yield dividends in an uncertain future. Openness is productive.

But suppose in spite of, even because of, the best efforts of leadership an enterprise doesn't survive. We live in times of aggressive,
predatory competition, in an age of mergers, acquisitions, restructurings
and deconstructions. No enterprise can rule out forever the possibility
that one day it may lose its identity. Shall we then describe this as
success or failure? To answer, perhaps we need a word of wisdom
(there should be little argument with the proposition that our future
enterprises will need not only competent leaders but wise leaders).

Dr Edward de Bono, world authority in the direct teaching of
thinking as a skill, has this to say in *Edward de Bono's Textbook
of Wisdom*:

> Wisdom is more about perspective than about detail. Cleverness is
> about how we get information and how we use information.
> Wisdom is about how the information fits into the world around
> and our own values.
>
> Wisdom is to do with the broader view. Wisdom is to do with
> the deeper view. Wisdom is to do with the richer view. Wisdom
> seeks to take the 'helicopter view', so that everything can be seen in
> perspective and in relation to everything else.

James McBride's words chosen to introduce this reflection are words of wisdom, quarried from lives, his mother's and his own, of great hardship yet greater hope. Wisdom always invites us to stand where we can see beyond our fences and defences to the light on the far hill.

So I conclude with two stories which have added life and light to my more mundane endeavours.

In the recent past, I have attended two small retirement dinners for long-serving Baulderstone employees. Each retiree had close to 40 years of service, each was retiring from a senior management position, each had started work as an apprentice carpenter. The 20 or so guests invited in each case mostly had long service with the company and presented a diverse cross-section of experience and leadership. It was to be expected that conversation would turn to telling old stories.

Part of the enjoyment I gained from these occasions came from hearing, often for the first time, some recollections about the company and its activities, and about individual incidents and exchanges from the perspective of others who had been involved. The years, perhaps, had added a notch or two of frankness to the mostly humorous and good-natured reminiscences! A consequence of listening is always to learn something. Anecdotes of relationships between the people in various project offices were always to the fore and usually added an earthy dimension to teamwork practised compared with teamwork professed. What I learnt continued to keep my feet firmly on the ground about how much progress Baulderstone had made towards the ideal of becoming an excellent enterprise.

But if there were different perspectives and assessments about progress, there was also a strong bond of mutual respect and trust between us all for we had all grown and learned much from being part of our shared experience. We were not the same people as we would have been otherwise.

The second illustration came when, in November 1998, I received an unexpected letter with another story from the past and the present. It was from a director of nursing at the aged-care institution I mentioned and recalled a patient whom she had first met as a trainee nurse.

In 1975, Baulderstone was contracted to build a nine-storey new wing at the Home for Incurables [now The Julia Farr Centre]. Everyday for the next eighteen months a patient by the name of Lennie would spend his days watching the building project. Lennie was a rich man – despite his physical and intellectual handicaps, he was rich because he owned a Baulderstone hard hat. That hard hat, given to Lennie by the foreman on the site, was Lennie's most precious possession. He wore it everyday for as many years as I remember knowing him. Lennie has continued to supervise many building projects from his wheelchair. His life had meaning because of his Baulderstone hat. Lennie is still alive, his only possessions are his wheelchair and his hat which he still wears every day.

Ripples on a pond. Experiences which portray the fruitfulness of openness and open-heartedness. Experiences which bring encouragement to keep an enterprise moving on a pathway towards excellence.

BIBLIOGRAPHY

Blake, Robert R., Avis, Warren E. and Mouton, Jane S., *Corporate Darwinism*, Gulf Publishing Co., Houston, Texas, 1966

Blake, Robert R. and Mouton Jane S., *Making Experience Work: The Grid Approach to Critique*, McGraw Hill Book Co., 1978

Blake, Robert R. and Mouton, Jane S., *The Managerial Grid III – The Key to Leadership Excellence*, Gulf Publishing Company, Houston, 1985

Collins, James C. and Porras, Jerry I., *Built to Last: Successful Habits of Visionary Companies*, Century, London, 1994

Conrad, Joseph, *Lord Jim*, Penguin Books Ltd, London, 1900

Cracknell, Ruth, *A Biased Memoir*, Viking, Penguin Books, Australia, 1997

De Bono, Edward, *Edward De Bono's Textbook of Wisdom*, Penguin Books, 1996

Donovan, Peter F., *Towards Excellence: The A.W. Baulderstone Story*, Pagel Books for A.W. Baulderstone Holdings Pty Ltd, Adelaide, 1987

Drucker, Peter F., *The New Realities: In Government and Politics/In Economics and Business/In Society and World View*, Harper & Row, New York, 1989

Frick, Don M. and Spears, Larry C., (eds), *On Becoming a Servant Leader: The Private Writings of Robert K Greenleaf*, Jossey-Bass, San Francisco, 1996

Greenleaf, Robert K., *Servant Leadership: A Journey into the Nature of Legitimate Power and Greatness*, Paulist Press, New York, 1977

Homer, *The Odyssey*, translated by Robert Fitzgerald, The Franklin Library, 1979

McBride, James, *The Colour of Water*, Hodder Headline Australia, 1997

McKay, Hugh, *Generations – Baby Boomers, their parents and their children*, Pan Macmillan, Australia, 1997

May, Rollo, *The Courage to Create*, W.W. Norton & Co., New York, 1975

Plato: Selected Dialogues, Quoted from 'Crito', The Translation of Benjamin Jowett, The Franklin Library

Taylor, Charles, *The Ethics of Authenticity*, Harvard University Press, 1991

Tillich, Paul, *Love, Power and Justice*, Oxford University Press, 1954

Tournier, Paul, MD, *The Healing of Persons*, Harper & Row, New York, 1967

Tuchman, Barbara, *The Proud Tower: A Portrait of the World before the War 1890–1914*, The Macmillan Company, New York, 1966

West, Morris, *Cassidy*, Hodder & Stoughton, 1986

INDEX

Wakefield Press has been publishing good Australian books
for over fifty years. For a catalogue of current and
forthcoming titles, or to add your name to our mailing list,
send your name and address to

Wakefield Press, Box 2266, Kent Town, South Australia 5071.

TELEPHONE (08) 8362 8800 FAX (08) 8362 7592
WEB www.wakefieldpress.com.au

ARTSA

Wakefield Press thanks Wirra Wirra Vineyards and Arts South Australia
for their continued support.